'Tapped Out'

A Worker's Memoir of Bethlehem Steel's Rise and Demise in Western New York

Michael D. Langan

digital@batesjackson llc

ON THE COVER: AN OPEN HEARTH FURNACE AT BETHLEHEM STEEL'S LACKAWANNA PLANT IS "TAPPED OUT". THE PROCESS ENABLES STEEL TO RUN FROM THE FURNACE INTO THE LADLE. NOTE THE SLAG RUNNING INTO THE "SLAG POT" LOWER LEFT.
Photo: Steelways Magazine, Bethlehem Steel.

ISBN. 978-1-932583-49-6
Copyright© 2010 Michael D. Langan

Printed and bound in the USA by

17-21 elm street
buffalo, ny 14203
716.854.3000 phone
716.847.1965 fax
www.batesjackson.com

This book is dedicated to the men and women who worked at the Lackawanna, New York plant of Bethlehem Steel.

TABLE OF CONTENTS

Introduction

This is the story of the rise and demise of Bethlehem Steel in Lackawanna. In it, I write about what the plant meant to me and to those I knew who saw it as a promise of work and a career.

When Bethlehem Steel left Lackawanna in 1982, it was the end of an era in America, a time of tumult that lasted most of the 20th century.

As a steelworker at Lackawanna's Bethlehem plant from 1955 - 1963, I shared a part of the excitement of making steel. Equally, I was disappointed when the company disappeared from the scene about twenty years later. Bethlehem was like the Cheshire cat - cue its mischievous grin - that, upon disappearing, left a gaping economic hole in the Western New York community.

Do you remember the classical description of a steel mill? " … a broad mix of occupations and workers, skilled, semi-skilled and unskilled; Black, white, Latinos; ethnics and WASPS; precision workers and assembly-line workers; backbreaking labor and light machine work; outside and inside work; transporting, shipping, fabrication, forging, smelting, constructing; simple mechanical and sophisticated computer processes; it's all there in an integrated steel plant..."[1]

It may have been 'all there' in my mind, but I have waited a long time to write about Bethlehem Steel's Lackawanna Plant, #2 open hearth. (Bethlehem built the last 'integrated' plant at Burns Harbor, Indiana in 1962.)

It is 55 years and I am semi-deep in retirement before putting my thoughts to paper. My excuses for not writing earlier are the usual, marrying, raising a family and earning a living.

The open hearth, however, has never been out of my thoughts. It was a huge, fiery, dangerous, forbidding place. Every day I went to work, I thought about the odds of not coming home. It was a place of excitement, with the drama of a heat of steel tapping out, as well as the rough and tumble of learning the job with older, experienced men making steel. That was a big deal to me then - and now.

In fact, 'tapped out' is a phrase that takes on meaning beyond emptying a furnace of a heat of steel. The expression 'tapped out' comes from the third helper on a furnace 'tapping' the gong at the back of his furnace. This notice of impending alarm was made prior to the second helper actually 'tapping' the heat of steel.

'Tapping or hitting the gong' at the back of the furnace had a clear meaning. It was meant to warn workers on the pit-side of the furnace of an impending explosion of metal that could shoot across the pit before settling into the ladle. In plain language, it meant, "Get your butt out of the way or get killed."

'Tapped Out' is also a phrase that means 'shot', 'beat-to-hell' and worn out. (More broadly, in private conversations among old time furnace workers, it signified a woman who delivered a child.) Moreover, to continue the analogy, with the birth of a child, there was relief and expectation. However, a child's developmental progress does not always accord with parents' wishes. Bethlehem's leaving Lackawanna certainly did not comport with the workers' and community's desires.

'Tapped out' in the open hearth had that extended meaning about life in general, suggesting there was nothing left to anticipate. In that sense, 'tapped out' describes Bethlehem Steel at the end of its days.

I should acknowledge that the association of my family with steel making began long before me, but I knew little about it. I began my work at Bethlehem as a laborer in the open hearth and, in time, became a salaried worker lighting open-hearth furnaces and taking turns as a foreman. My reliance upon the plant started with needing tuition money while attending Canisius College, but it went beyond that. I enjoyed the work and being a steelworker. Like me, many students 55 years ago were able to find jobs at the plant. Not any more.

As a result, this is also a story about something that largely has ceased to exist in the United States in the 21st century: laboring in a huge factory environment. I try to tell some of the company and plant history as well as stories about people I knew who shared the Bethlehem experience and what impact it had on them.

In the years that I worked there and after, Bethlehem Steel was a spur to the local economy in Lackawanna and Buffalo - and a help to those who sought work - either as a temporary balm or as a long-term career.

'Tapped Out' indicates the sense of loss that Bethlehem's employees and retirees felt after Bethlehem announced the end of steelmaking in December 1982. The company lost $100 million at the Lackawanna plant in 1981. Bethlehem executives gave this and other reasons for the company's failure. Their thinking was understandable but not compelling because senior executives themselves helped to bring the company down.

In fact, reasons for Bethlehem's failure were legion: excessive and foolhardy spending on the part of the corporation, lack of foresight about the competitiveness of global steel production, union demands and City of Lackawanna hyper-taxation among them.

No matter how you think about it, 'reasons' don't speak to the pain experienced by workers who spent part of their working lives there. How could they? Discomfort is writ large for workers in an American steel industry that is a shadow of its former self. Not only that, the loss of "promise" to young people that a career in steel once afforded also disappeared.

Today, little of the industry remains in the traditional sense. Mini-mills, generally small production operations, are the name of the game.

If you have any doubt, witness the drop off in employment. Jobs in the steel industry declined "... from 2.5 million in 1974 to less than a million in 1998. Global production stood at 773 million tons in 1997, down from 786 million tons in 1988. U.S. steel production has remained constant since the 1970s at about 100 million tons, but 50% of that total is now produced by mini-mill companies."[2]

By June 1, 2010, *The Wall Street Journal* reported that "The world's steel mills are ramping up production so quickly that prices in some markets are expected to fall 5% or more in June...while prices have remained relatively strong in Europe and the U.S., in part because many idled mills haven't been restarted."[3]

That sense of loss - imports now account for 25 percent of all steel used in the United States annually - has spread throughout an American economy that is beginning to cede its prominence to other countries' global efforts.

My hope is that this book gives insight into an industrial era in America now gone. "The furnaces are cold, the forges silent."[4] Is there any doubt that Bethlehem and its promise of a productive life for workers has 'tapped out'?

'Tapped Out'
Chapter 1: Postcards from the Past

A good deal of family history preceded my taking a job as a steel worker at Bethlehem Steel's Lackawanna Plant open hearths in 1955. At the time, I didn't know about any of it. The story goes back two generations to my mother's grandfather, Mike Laffey, at the turn of the 20th century.

Times have changed since then. Today we text each other, use iPhones, BlackBerries and other devices unimaginable to people a little over a century ago.

Recently, using a more old-fashioned method, analyzing family post cards, I tried to find out when and why my grandparents, my mother's parents, Mike Laffey and Beatrice Lally Laffey, came from Scranton, PA to Lackawanna, NY around the year 1900.

I'm not certain, but I think that Mike Laffey moved to find a job with the Lackawanna Iron and Steel Company as it transferred its equipment from Scranton to West Seneca, NY, in 1899.

Practically speaking, how does one find out what happened 110 years ago, 'connecting the dots' as we now say? What is left to be analyzed? Certainly, letters might be reviewed, if there were any. In this case, none exists that I know of.

Instead, I have a few postcards. That's right, postcards. My aunt, Jean Laffey, my mother's sister, who died in the late 1970s, left me some family post-cards from the early 1900s. Most people wrote post-cards to each other at the turn of the 20th century. You might have thought that people communicated by phone in 1900, since it had been invented more than twenty-five years earlier. However, there weren't many phones installed in private residences. They cost too much.

On the other hand, mail delivery in 1900 was usually twice a day in the United States, and cheap - a penny a card. If you lived in the same town, Scranton, PA, for example, you could count on your friend receiving your card and the friend sending a return 'pc' the same day. I mention this because it highlights the importance of postcards as a form of communication more than one hundred years ago.

It is not clear from the postcards I examined whether Mike Laffey knew my grandmother, Beatrice Lally in Scranton, or whether they met and married in Lackawanna. I checked to see if they married in Scranton, PA. No luck. I searched marriage records in the clerk's offices of Lackawanna, West Seneca and Buffalo, but found no record of their marriage there, either.

I continue to search and discover a few facts that argue against what I earlier thought - that Beatrice Lally was born in Scranton. In fact, she may have been born in the Buffalo area.

Ancestors' research can be complicated, although Internet search engines now make it easier. To begin with, it was not until 1914 that many states required the recordation of births, marriages and deaths as public records. Before that time, many families noted major events like these in their family bibles.

This is probably what my grandparents did. Many young couples did not have money or transportation to travel to an office of vital records at some distance to make a record of something that had already taken place and for which there was no legal requirement.

These record-keeping issues make it hard to find out my grandfather's relationship, if any, to Bethlehem Steel. In those years, people - particularly uneducated men - normally did not record what they considered daily happenstance in a diary. So how might I know more about them today? The options are limited. Where would you look for people long dead? You guessed it, the cemetery.

I called Holy Cross Cemetery in Lackawanna, NY, on February 2, 2010. I spoke with a helpful employee named Linda. I asked her, after giving the appropriate data, "Were my grandfather, Mike Laffey, and his wife, Beatrice, buried there?"

Linda put me on hold and went away to check out my query. Minutes went by while I waited, via the phone. She came back and gave me great information about both of them. First, Michael Laffey died April 8, 1934 at 60 years and 5 months of age.

This information, tied to data I gleaned the same day from the Church of Latter Day Saints' Internet site, indicates that a Michael T. Laffey was born in Allegheny County, PA in 1874. I am quite sure that Mike Laffey was my grandfather.

The Allegheny PA record, (copied by the Mormons), noted that Mike's father, probably my great-great-grandfather, also named Michael Laffey, was born in Pennsylvania in 1850.

This earlier Mike Laffey was by occupation a 'puddler', a job involved in 19th century steel making that required considerable skill. His father, likely my great-grandfather, was born in Ireland, according to the Allegheny ledger. Thus, the earlier Laffeys must have migrated from Ireland in the 1840s, a time of consecutive potato crop devastations that took hundreds of thousands of lives.

Mike's occupation, 'Puddling' was part of an Industrial Revolution means of making iron and steel. In the original puddling technique, molten iron in a reverberatory furnace was stirred with rods, which were consumed in the process.

Later, it was also used to produce a good-quality steel with the correct amount of carbon; this was a highly skilled art, but both high-carbon and low-carbon steels were successfully produced on a small scale, particularly for swords, knives and other weapons.[5] Steel making, it seemed, was in the blood of the Laffey family, forging and reinforcing - however unknown to me - my relationship with Bethlehem.

Mike, the 'puddler', owed his occupation to a Welch immigrant, David Thomas, who "… established himself as a pioneer of America's Industrial Revolution. It was he who developed the all important 'coke' used in blast furnaces, working for Lehigh Crane, which had a few hundred men on the payroll. He fired up the first commercially successful anthracite-fueled iron furnace in America, producing 4 tons of iron on the Fourth of July 1840, at Lehigh Crane Iron Co. in Catasauqua, Pa.. Iron making swept the Lehigh Valley.[6]

David Thomas left Lehigh Crane in 1854, to "... begin his own ironworks, the Thomas Iron Co...Pig iron furnaces began transforming rural landscapes..." The groundbreaking work of these two companies and Thomas' leadership laid the framework for Bethlehem Steel.[7]

These few historical "stokes" into the ironworking furnaces give a sense of the story behind the development of the steel industry in the United States.

Now let me get back to my conversation with Linda at Holy Cross Cemetery: "Could you tell me anything about my grandmother, Beatrice Laffey?" I asked.

Once more, Linda said, "Please hold," and away she went again to check records.

Linda returned to the phone and said, "Yes, Beatrice Laffey, died on June 8, 1929, age 50. Our record shows that she was born in Buffalo. But this may not be so," Linda said, "... as the record is hand-written. "Sometimes people who are grieving either misspeak or do not know and assume the deceased was local."

Linda's words are a big surprise to me. I had thought all along that Beatrice was born in Scranton, PA. When I checked the PA birth records, however, I could not find her birth record, not altogether surprising. Still, I wonder if the notation about her Buffalo birth is accurate. In the middle of the Great Depression, an uninformed or distracted family member may have given inaccurate information.

Beatrice Lally Laffey's birth record in Buffalo is not recorded. It may have been noted in a family bible, long ago discarded. However, I continue to try to locate a marriage record of my grandparents as a matter of thoroughness.

In my search for their marriage record, I talk to Msgr. Dave Gallivan, a long-time friend, who suggests that I contact Msgr. Paul J.E. Burkard, Pastor of Our Lady of Victory National Shrine. He suggests that I call Queen of Angels Rectory at 144 Warsaw Street in Lackawanna. This rectory keeps the records of St. Barbara's and St. Hyacinth's Churches, both now closed. I check out this source, mentioning that the marriage likely took place sometime between

1900 and 1908. Result: nothing turns up.

What is clear is that Beatrice Lally, as an enterprising young woman, knew that she needed a job to help support herself. Eventually, too, she needed to find a husband. It takes no great leap of imagination to understand that women in Bea's situation, whether born in Buffalo or Scranton, would gravitate to where men pursuing work would travel, such as to the shore of Lake Erie south of Buffalo.

At the same time, I research Bethlehem Steel[8] and its antecedent, the Lackawanna Iron & Steel Company through other local publications. It seems likely that the plant's relocation influenced Mike Laffey and Beatrice Lalley Laffey's move to the First Ward, close by the plant, as indicated in an early postcard address.

Before moving to Lackawanna, however, the making of steel developed along what would later be called 'paradigm shift' lines, a phrase first used by Thomas Kuhn in his book, "The Structure of Scientific Revolutions", in 1962. The term gives a name to what had earlier taken place: a basic shift in approach to making steel. Part of the theory requires taking whatever steps assure the continuation of profits (no surprise), even if it means moving locus and changing the nature of production and the plants themselves. Big shots don't care about the little guys.

Some examples of development, reorganization and profit lines follow. In 1846, the Delaware, Lehigh, Schuylkill & Susquehanna Railroad was organized, renamed the Lehigh Valley Railroad in

1853. The line carried passengers and coal. In 1856, Augustus Wolle formed Bethlehem Steel's earliest ancestor, the Saucona Iron Company, to create anthracite-fueled iron works and the Cambria Iron Co., in Johnstown, revolutionized the production of iron rails. In 1859, Saucona Iron reorganized as Bethlehem Rolling Mill & Iron Co.

By 1862, Bethlehem reorganized as Bethlehem Iron Co., and its first blast furnace is "blown in" on July 17th, with puddling furnaces making wrought-iron blooms for the rolling mill, making it a major rail supplier. By 1873, Bethlehem was a success and it completed its first Bessemer plant, producing its first steel rails on October 4. In 1886, Bethlehem began forging hammers, presses, ordnance, and armor plate for the Navy, beginning its long history with America's defense industry. By 1888, Bethlehem's first battery of open-hearth furnaces began operation.

In 1892, steelworkers in the nation's largest craft union struck for better wages at the Carnegie Homestead Works near Pittsburgh. On July 6, strikers battled 300 security guards sent to protect non-union workers, called 'scabs.' Ten people were killed with Carnegie force carrying the day. Steelworkers, how-ever, did not give up. Workers followed the industry as it shifted from place to place in an effort to avoid unionization.

In 1899, Bethlehem Steel was created as a hold-ing company, with Bethlehem Iron as its only asset. Eugene G. Grace, later to run Bethlehem, joins the company as a crane operator. Former Carnegie Steel

President Charles M. Schwab becomes president of U.S. Steel Corp, buying Bethlehem Steel for himself for $7.2 million, and then sells it to J.P. Morgan, U.S. Steel's underwriter, for the same price.

Do you think this is complicated? Hold your breath, it gets worse. Two years later, Schwab buys back Bethlehem for $30 million in stocks and bonds, involving him in a scandal among high rollers who accuse him of arranging a competing company's failure to grab assets.[9] This deal makes today's futures' market look simple.

Now back to those postcards. They give some tantalizing hints about how men and women migrated from one place to another, following the prospect of work. One begins to see how the little man and his wife were pawns in a very great scheme of money-making by the uber-rich.

Case in point: the Scranton-based Lackawanna Iron and Steel Company decided to re-locate to West Seneca, N.Y.[10] in 1899. If one views the larger picture of the 'paradigm shift' in steelmaking, that is, the search for newer production methods, access to natural resources and ease of shipping steel products, it becomes clear why captains of industry were casting an eye in the direction of the Great Lakes and in particular, the Buffalo, N.Y. area.

The Lackawanna Diamond Jubilee Booklet (1909 - 1984)[11] indicates that as early as that year, 1899, "... there were rumors that a large industry was planning to locate along the lake shore." In that same year, the Lackawanna Iron & Steel Co. increased its capital from $3,750,000 to $25,000,000. Construction of the new mill, called the "Eighth Wonder of the World", began on May 29, 1900. By the end of the first year of the new century, 2,000 men worked at the plant. [12]

Why did the company move? One reason was the unionization of the company's coal and iron mines, organized by the United Mine Workers in 1897. Strikes followed, wages increased, the cost of shipping iron ore to Scranton was huge, and the company had no rail lines to connect with emerging markets.[13]

In addition, the owner of the company, William Walker Scranton, knew about the building of a 7,500-foot break wall constructed with money from the federal government at the eastern end of Lake Erie. "The southern arms of this break wall...extended to Stony Point in West Seneca and made the lake shore an ideal spot for industry." Scranton took advantage of it. The decision to move was his.

John J. Albright purchased all the land along the lakeshore for the new company, renamed the Lackawanna Steel Company in 1902. "By the spring of 1901, several large buildings were completed and the withdrawal from Scranton, had begun. Wherever possible both men and machines were removed from Scranton to the new plant site at Stony Point."[14]

The South Buffalo Railway entered into the action, as did owners of boatloads of ore, arriving the next year. Keep in mind that Scranton, had no access to water for shipping, and, the Lake Erie break wall was a huge advantage.

An uncle of mine, Johnny Timlin, was a diver who worked to construct the break wall south of Buffalo at the turn of the 20th century. I remember as a boy seeing his diving suit with its huge metal Jules Verne-type helmet propped up against the furnace in the cellar of the Timlin family home. Uncle Johnny, used to rough ways, slept on an army cot next to the furnace as an old man.

Given these advantages, Lackawanna Steel sensed success, reorganized and recapitalized to the tune of $60,000,000 in 1902, with Cornelius Vanderbilt among others on the board as backers. Giants of industry smelled success.

"The economic coup which William Walker Scranton had engineered did not please the board of directors, however, who replaced him in late 1904..." It may be that he ruffled too many feathers moving the company. The company's property in Scranton, PA was sold to the Wyoming Valley Railroad, which scrapped all the remaining equipment and tore down all the old buildings except for the oldest stone blast furnaces.[15] This hard lesson for a steel town, think Lackawanna, was to be suffered more than once in the 20th century.

Moreover, the new steel company had a rocky relationship with West Seneca, NY. The company wanted sewer, water, gas and road improvements but would not pay for them. Workers swelled the town's population and cholera, typhoid and influenza broke out. There was no housing of consequence. The Irish

POURING STEEL AT BETHLEHEM'S LACKAWANNA
STEEL PLANT, 1922.

immigrants likely said, "Bad cess," meaning, "a curse
upon you", a phrase also suggesting, 'lousy plumbing.'

West Seneca proposed separating the area around the steel mill, making it an incorporated municipality of its own, called Lackawanna, but the company objected. However, the steel company relented in 1909 after a two-year panic that nearly bankrupted the Town of West Seneca and threatened steel making.[16]

Lackawanna Steel experienced fractious times as it attempted to skirt unionization. Workers interested in a union followed the company from Scranton. Two decades later, in 1919, the company fired hundreds of workers because they were union members or sympathizers. Thousands of workers protested and on September 23, company police clashed with 3000 striking workers, killing two and injuring three.

Lackawanna Steel, earlier employing only 72 African Americans, retaliated against the union by hiring several thousand black strikebreakers and brought them to the city to maintain operations.[17]

Against this life of friction, prejudice and the hardship of no available work, many steel workers felt the need for religious consolation. Religion was the core of life for many of them. At this point, a prospective saint enters the picture. In 1882, Father Nelson Baker was in charge of St. Patrick's Church (1875 - 1921), built on Limestone Hill, where the present Our Lady of Victory Basilica stands.

Nelson Henry Baker was a veteran of the Union army, a successful businessman in Buffalo and, after a late vocation became a priest, studying at Our Lady of the Angels Seminary at Niagara University.

Bishop Ryan sent Father Baker to Limestone Hill in the spring of 1876. Father Baker worked at St. Patrick's for five years. At this point, the bishop transferred Baker to St. Mary's Parish in Corning, NY, where Baker 'renewed his strength.' It may be that Father Baker had some kind of physical or emotional breakdown. Life as a priest on Limestone Hill certainly wasn't easy.

Limestone Hill was a daunting challenge to which Nelson Baker returned in 1882, again at the request of the bishop, and he remained there, building up a great enterprise for the poor, the homes of charity that included St. Joseph's Orphanage and St. John's Protectory. (In time, because of the growing population and needs of the city due to the steel plant, Father Baker built the Basilica, the Infant Home, a hospital and school. He stayed at the parish of Our Lady of Victory, to whom he was devoted, until his death in 1936.)

By 1900, St. Patrick's parish was growing rapidly as work progressed on the construction of the steel plant along the shore of Lake Erie. "The transfer of the Lackawanna Steel and Iron Company to West Seneca involved the relocation of two thousand workers (of the plant's six thousand workers) from Scranton, Pennsylvania, the original site of the plant. Most of the new arrivals were Catholic...seeking employment at the new plant."

At this point, allow me to return to connecting the dots between grandparents and Bethlehem. As I earlier mentioned, my aunt, Jean Laffey gave me the old cards in 1977. They were family memorabilia, so Jean kept them. Some PCs were her mother's, Beatrice Laffey nee Lally, who received them where she lived first in Scranton, as a single girl, and later in Lackawanna, New York, as wife of my grandfather, Michael Laffey.

The cards reflect traceries of lost lives that I wish to know more about as they touch upon the Bethlehem experience.

The first postcard is from a 'Frances C', likely a girlfriend of Beatrice Lally as a young woman. She sends a card to her from Cortland, NY. The card shows a scene of Tompkins Street, looking west, in that small town, sent November 8, 1904. Underneath the picture, Frances writes, "Come back to Cortland. I am here. You can board with me at 169 Homer Ave. Bill has left town. So has Mr. (?) Answer soon. Frances C."

This card raises a number of questions. Who was Frances C? What were she and my grandmother doing in Cortland, rooming together at the turn of the last century? Were there jobs in Cortland that would have drawn young women from Scranton? Of course, there were jobs there.

If there were jobs in Lackawanna that drew men to leave one city and go to the mills in another, why not jobs in Cortland, NY to draw women? Why mightn't single women go together for a job to another city and room with one another? Moreover, who was 'Bill'? What about the mysterious 'Mr. (?)'? Who knows? These women were reserved and did not tell everything they knew on postcards.

These cards demonstrate that young women needed two things - a job and a husband. The postcards and their modest references to the importance of beaux coyly point this out.

I checked Google Maps on the Internet and there appears still to be a 169 Homer Avenue address in Cortland.[18] When I looked into the history of Cortland around 1900, I found that by 1855, 10 percent of the city's residents were born in Ireland. Two railroads lines ran through the town, one laid down in 1854 and a second in 1872.

In addition, there were three banks and a number of small enterprises, such as the Cortland Wagon Company, the largest of a dozen firms making horse-drawn vehicles. Wickwire Brothers turned from hardware to wire and nails. It was the largest area employer. Cortland shipped butter and cheese to the East Coast. Surely, it seems that young women like Frances C. and Beatrice Lalley could take a train from Scranton to Cortland in pursuit of work.

The next card received by my grandmother thickens the mystery. "Frances C" has moved to Dover, NJ. Why would she have gone there? Again, she might have been pursuing work, perhaps, like many young Irish women, as a housemaid or a nanny.

A history of Morris County (NJ) indicates, "By 1900 the nation's business and financial leaders, seeking escape from New York City...discovered Morris County, its isolation, ideal climate and unspoiled countryside, and started the construction of large country estates.

Within a few years, it was claimed that more millionaires lived within a one-mile radius of the Morristown Green than elsewhere in the world. The fabulous estates were numerous enough to fill the pages of a pre-World War I vintage picture book entitled *Beautiful Homes of Morris County*. Possibly the most opulent were those of Otto H. Kahn, Hamilton McK. Twombly, Charles Mellon, etc."[19]

Frances writes to my grandmother on July 28, 1906, in a faded script alongside a photo of a body of water in Dover called Black Pond: "Received your letter. Was glad to hear from you. Why did you leave Cortland?" I may come back. Will you send me some postals from Scranton? Frances."

It's unclear whether Frances meant to return to Cortland or to Scranton. Why would she want some postcards from Scranton? Perhaps she was lonely.

The next card to my grandmother, dated August 19, 1906, is from another correspondent, "A. Fisk." It is a black and white photo of a boating scene on the Tioughnioga, in Homer, NY, near Cortland.

The message does not encourage one to travel to Homer. It reads, "Nothing doing. Cooney has got another girl." Why would my grandmother care about this Edwardian cad Cooney? Perhaps he was an old beau. Again, husband-hinting information is given.

Next comes a card dated August 30, 1906, showing West Blackwell St., Dover, N.J. from my mother's correspondent, Frances C, who now signs herself "F.E.G.C."

She writes, "Dear Beatrice, Just returned from a two-week's visit to New York and Brooklyn. Meant to send you some postals from there but forgot to take your address with me. How about going back to Cortland? Will you go if I will? See Mr. Mc L - and get your place back. I am dying to get back to see "Little - G." Answer and let me know."

Apparently, 'Mr. Mc L' was the owner of the boarding house. Who was "Little - G"? Did Beatrice and Frances have jobs in Cortland at one point, rooming together at the boarding house? It seems so.

The next postcard is dated July 12, 1909 from "Kate." It shows a cat on a fence that has eaten a bird, saying "I've had a 'bird' of a time." Perhaps Kate visited my grandmother at 2302 Pittston Avenue in Scranton. (The Pittston address still exists on Google Maps today. I remember staying in that house with my Aunt Sabina, a sister of Beatrice, during WW II.)

Three years pass before the next card. Beatrice Lally has become Mrs. Michael Laffey. I don't know the date of their wedding. I suspect that they married sometime between 1907 and 1909.

She and her husband lived at 223 First St., Lackawanna, NY. This address is long gone. However, I have a good idea of where the house was located. This is thanks to Mike Malyak, who worked at Bethlehem in the 50s and 60s. He is Secretary/Treasurer of The Steel Plant Museum, Inc., and a retired teacher who serves as a docent at the Bethlehem Steel Museum in the lower level of the Lackawanna Public Library.

Malyak, a font of information, says that the address was located approximately in the middle of the block, between the Hamburg Turnpike and A Street, on the south side. This side of the block ran from structures numbering 200 to 252.

First Street was part of a neighborhood built for workers near Bethlehem Steel called Old Village, according to Mr. Malyak. In the museum there is a diagram of the layout of the village and a drawing by Walter Sanok, now deceased, who lived there. The fact that my grandfather and grandmother lived in the Old Village seem to argue for Mike Laffey working at the plant, though I don't know this with certainty.

The history of the City of Lackawanna makes clear Bethlehem's self-interest in building housing for workers near the plant.

Almost as soon as work began (on the construction of the plant) the company contracted for the erection of two housing projects known as the Old Village and the New Village. The first (or "Old Village") provided more than 400 row-type brick apartments which, while lacking individuality, were far superior to other rental properties and considerably less expensive. Each apartment had four or five rooms, interior plumbing, and sewage disposal, and at $7.50 per month should have been fully occupied.

The town of West Seneca and the Limestone Hill area, later to become Lackawanna, built up around the burgeoning number of newcomers.

"Commercial activity kept pace with the

expanding plant. Certainly, the boarding houses and saloons abounded. Ridge Road could boast of Lenham's Mercantile Company, a good-sized general store, built in 1902; Skudwick's Drug Store at Gates Avenue; Hedley & Whalen Hardware Company on Ingram Avenue; the O'Mara Building housing and the U.S. Post Office in 1907 ... Young's Drug Store, 1905; at Ridge and South Park; George Avery's plumbing shop, 1905; ... the Lackawanna National Bank, 1904." Besides those on the main drag, "there were many neighborhood stores throughout..."

The area was taking on an urban aspect, "... with trolley cars on Ridge Road, South Park, and Electric avenues. Sidewalks and pavement were still in the future."[20] My other grandfather, Tom Langan, was an early conductor on the trolley car that ran from Blasdell up Electric Avenue, to Ridge Road until October 2, 1941.

This description of major activity in and around Lackawanna, is the context of a postcard sent to Lackawanna from Mike Laffey's sister, Maria. It shows a maid sitting in a garden surrounded with fragrant flowers. A handsome man watches the maiden, thinking her quite the prettiest flower in the scene.

The card is postmarked from Scranton, June 30, 1912. Maria writes: "Dear Brother and Wife, I will leave Scranton Wednesday June the 3 at 6:18 in the morning do not forget to meet me on the 1:05 in Buffalo. Good bye. Maria."

Maria, Mike's sister, is on her way. In the meantime, Beatrice is a wife with plenty to do.

What happened? Likely, she met her future husband, Mike Laffey, and in time they moved to Lackawanna as he looked for work. Beatrice and Mike had four children, probably born between 1909 and 1916; namely and in order of birth, Cyril, Jean, Catherine (my mother) in 1913 and John (Babe).

Whether or not Mike Laffey worked at Bethlehem, his sons Cyril and Babe both did for a time, as did my father, Eugene T. Langan, and his brothers, Francis (Franny) and Manus Langan. It was the promise of jobs at Bethlehem that made growing to manhood in Lackawanna, in those years from 1900 to 1940, tolerable. If you could get a job, it meant prosperity and a chance for a future.

I don't know much about my grandfather, Mike Laffey. My mother and her siblings didn't talk about their parents. I know that Mike played semi-pro and perhaps professional baseball as a catcher. He umpired local games. Again, my mother said it was whispered that he took bribes to make the 'right' calls. Who knows the value of gossip?

Her father, Mike, my mother told me, knew Babe Ruth, because they both came from Pennsylvania, where Ruth played in the minor leagues. Ruth, of course, was not born until 1895. Mike Laffey and Babe Ruth must have become friends after 1915, the time Ruth was breaking into the big leagues.

Mike tried to take Cyril, his oldest, to meet the Babe when he was visiting Buffalo in the 1920s, when Cyril was about ten. "Who cares about meeting

"The Babe"? Cyril is supposed to have said. Cyril had no interest in baseball and wouldn't go to the Hotel Lafayette, where the Babe was staying, according to Nellie Rooney, a maid at the Lafayette, who lived with us after her husband died on their honeymoon. Cyril's recalcitrance made his father furious.

Meantime, Cyril grew apace and was beaten up and arrested by the police for 'twirling' at the Dellwood Ballroom in downtown Buffalo as a young man. "Twirling", a dance activity seemingly harmless to me, involved swinging one's partner around in a grandiose and careless way, potentially injurious to others on the floor. It was illegal at the time. The reader can see where Cyril's interests lay. He certainly did not do any twirling when he worked at Bethlehem Steel, other than perhaps to avoid an overhead crane.

Cyril's father, Mike, had an interest in gardening, working at that job for one of the 'presidents' of Canisius College, Father Michael Ahern, SJ, who was Rector in the early 1920s. All this was told me by my mother, Catherine R. Langan. Family lore says that a truckload of whiskey hit and killed Mike on a dark night one year after Prohibition ended. He died on April 8, 1934, identified by his broken fingers, the result of being a catcher without much stuffing in his mitt.

To punctuate what I said earlier, my grandmother, Beatrice Lally Laffey, died before her husband on June 8, 1929, at the height of the Great Depression. She was only 50.

My mother and her brothers and sisters are gone now too. Catherine died in 1981, the others earlier.

But in 1904, this freighted history was 'future tense' for my maternal grandmother, Beatrice Lally, as she began saving treasured postcards from the edge of a past, largely unknown but ripe for more investigation - with its ties to Bethlehem Steel - that continues today.

POSTCARD FROM MARIA LAFFEY'S SISTER. IT WAS SENT FROM SCRANTON, PA TO LACKAWANNA, NY ON OR ABOUT JUNE 20, 1912. SHE WRITES TO MIKE (MY GRANDFATHER); DEAR BROTHER, I WILL LEAVE SCRANTON WEDNESDAY, JUNE THE 3 AT 6:18 IN THE MORNING. DO NOT FORGET TO MEET ME ON THE 1:05 IN BUFFALO. GOOD BY, MARIA.

Chapter 2: Growing Up in the 40s

Growing up in Lackawanna in the 1940s was an idyllic time - if you didn't know any better. Men and women had jobs at Bethlehem, while many spouses were away in the war. As a result, a community of parents and neighbors pitched in to lend each other a hand raising their young. Nobody was rich but we all got along.

The city had a population of about 24,000 people. Folks lived in small neighborhoods and knew each other. I wrote a reflection about that seemingly simpler time and stealing grapes as a kid in *The Buffalo News*.[21]

"Fall is the time of year that Concord grapes are gathered in Western New York, growing as they do on the hillsides of Lakes Erie and Ontario and the Finger Lakes, farther to the east. The grapes are a deep ecclesiastical purple and are my favorite fruit.

My wife and I set out some for breakfast the other day. While plucking the grapes from their reticent, lacy network of vine, I remembered something completely forgotten for perhaps 65 years.

I don't know what scientists call it when a taste,

or scent, or other physical sign triggers long-forgotten recollections, but as I popped a big purple grape in my mouth, I thought of my boyhood gang, the Apple Street Worms.

We all lived on Apple Street in Lackawanna. I don't think we thought of ourselves being called that in any derogatory way. It seemed apt in 1945.

Stealing Concord grapes was an activity of my gang when I was a boy. I was the ringleader, the big night crawler himself. The grapes were one of our nocturnal prizes, as we jumped from garage rooftop to garage rooftop and over back fences on our midnight surveys in the early fall darkness.

My sense of what was right and wrong is very clear on the grapes' caper. It was wrong, but with mitigating circumstances. I am not too regretful, as it involved 8-year-olds eating fruit in what seemed like the Garden of Eden at the time.

At the time I don't think it ever occurred to me that what we were doing was wrong or that it hurt anyone. It was a thrill to get home from Franklin Elementary School, change clothes, do homework, chores, have dinner and then go outside. Kids didn't get kidnapped in those days. Mother or dad would call me in by 8:30 or 9 p.m. But sometimes, especially on Friday or Saturday, I'd stay out later.

I remember one Friday night that our gang met together in the middle of a big field on Electric Avenue. We brought some potatoes from home along with whittled sticks, some clay and matches. We started a good fire, wrapped our potatoes in the clay, so that they wouldn't burn up on us, and crouched down around the fire in the darkness, probably the way cave men did, eons earlier.

We would squat there, smoking our pretend-cigarettes of matted field grass, with potatoes bobbing up and down, cooking over the fire as the night sky lit up with stars and the sparks we were making.

It is a glorious memory. What more could a boy want? It was fun to be a member of a gang, because it guaranteed having friends. "Gang" had a different meaning then than it does now. It meant a warm, companionable group of kids who enjoyed being together. Mickey Carter, Jackie Delaney, Paul Cavanaugh and me. We would shove each other around, crack jokes and enjoy our simple fare of burnt field grass and scorched potatoes.

It was from this small encampment that we would plan a sortie, going from garage rooftop to garage rooftop and yard-to-yard. When we got to the right garden, we'd spy our delectable grapes; swoop down like hawks on the prey, handling the forbidden fruit with dirty fingers and voracious mouths.

As I think about this episode now, as one who owns property, I'd go after those darned kids and kick their butts for their stealing. Thus does time revise our priorities.

Now, if I want some Concord grapes or a baked potato, I order them at a restaurant and complain about the price. Not only that, but I'm not sure that they taste as good as the ones out in the field, all those years ago."

In those years, Lackawanna had taverns on almost every corner, like Elmer Schatzel's across from Apple Street on Electric Avenue, and Curley's, located on Electric and Ridge Road, just up the street from Elmer's. Curly, the owner, was bald.

There was a candy and ice cream shop run by a Greek family, Economou's. And across Ridge Road and up half a block was the Colonial Kitchen, a dining room and take out run by Italian Nick Mattucci, who owned a farm south of Lackawanna, from which he took produce to the restaurant.

Almost next to the Colonial Kitchen was Osborne's Men's Wear, run by Billy Osborne, brother to Jack, who was principal of Lackawanna High School for decades. The Salem family, whose son Ed was a friend of mine at Father Baker High, were competitors of Osborne's, running men and women's stores nearby.

Joynt's was a bit of a dump where you could eat, if you were tough. A rump of beef and attendant flies sat and buzzed respectively in the window for a longer time than health officials might have allowed, if there were any health officials.

You could get a cup of coffee for a dime at the South Ridge Restaurant on the corner of South Park and Ridge. Across the Streets were Cord's Pharmacy and Our Lady of Victory Basilica, the center of town. The Limestone Grill, an historical artifact, was close by, populated by habitués of drink in retirement.

Back toward St. Barbara's Church, a Polish parish, on Ridge Road, Gene the Barber, had a shop that cut hair for 25 cents. The Post Office and the Franklin Theater were on either side of Gene's. In the 1940s, you could go to the movie for 9 cents. Witerski's market, Luke's market, Jacob's shoe repair and other groceries populated Electric Avenue near 29 Apple Street, where I lived.

I hope you can see from what I describe that Lackawanna was alive and bustling.

Fast forward ten years: Lackawanna was a small place in the 1950's, with all that such a designation entailed. When people got laid off, or hired, everybody knew about it.

The South Buffalo Railroad idled 11,000 employees, shutting down Bethlehem on April 30, 1950. "Fourteen rookie cops began their tours of duty in April 1951, as Chief Kubisty's department totaled 64."[22] My father was one of the rookie cops after WW II.

Places, events and people come to mind from that period. Rosinski's Furniture, a staple in my life as I passed it on Ridge Road every day, closed. L. B. Smith's Plaza in the 4th Ward opened in October 1951. Loblaw's new store in that plaza burned down on September 7, 1952.

Mayor John J. Janiga won a third term as Mayor in 1953, and a man I knew as a child, Chief Quinn of the Fire Department, retired. The Chief came from

Scranton with the old Lackawanna Iron & Steel Company, joining the force in 1914, when there were 15 men and 4 horses available to douse fires.

****

Childhood and innocence end. It did for me. I began taking odd jobs while I was still in elementary school. I checked hats and coats at the Hotel Lackawanna. Later, I cut grass at Holy Cross Cemetery and cleaned classrooms at Father Baker High School.

Certainly, being raw and inexperienced prompts one to take chances. As a result, I didn't think twice about saying 'yes' to the first job ever offered me, checking coats in the Hotel Lackawanna after WW II. It was 1949, and I was in seventh grade.

Joe Mescall, the dapper, bow-tied owner of the hotel, asked me if I'd like the job on Friday and Saturday nights, 6 p.m. to midnight or later. I'm sure my mother, who worked at the Hotel, was behind the offer. There were weddings, doctors' parties and other events that required a coat service on weekends. I was glad for the work.

To prepare for my new job, I took the IRC bus downtown and went to Ulbrich's Stationers. I borrowed ten dollars from my mother to buy a few hundred of the triplicate slips coat checkers used. There I got the slips: one to hand to the customer, another for the coat hanger and the last to insert into a hat. If it snowed or rained, I'd make up a fourth, a paper slip, and drop it into the winter footwear.

My uncle Babe Laffey and his sisters, Jean and my mother, Catherine, worked at the Hotel Lackawanna. Each got the other a job, starting with Babe, then Jean, and finally my mother. The old four-story building was *terra firma* to me. Babe was a bartender in the lounge for years. He served steelworkers from Bethlehem Steel, daily customers, until he died.

Tommy Clifford, one of Father Baker's orphan boys grown to manhood, rented a room at the hotel for years, and worked at Bethlehem as a conductor on the South Buffalo Railroad. After work, Tommy would stop into the bar. The bar was adjacent to the front desk. Tommy would order a 10-cent draft of Phoenix Beer, and chat with my uncle Babe. He did this for years. Decades later, Tom died in his sleep at the Hotel, the consequence of smoking in bed.

Andy Meddler, a friendly little man with bowed-legs and a Dickensian name, was the desk clerk. He would chat with me from time to time, while I worked in the cloakroom, situated alongside the marbled front desk. (Cloakroom is a wonderful ancient word, but no one ever dropped off a cloak while I collected outer garments there.) Jean and my mother waited on table in the dining room for lunch and dinner.

A thin little Puerto Rican man named Johnny, a heavy drinker with a red, mottled face, took care of maintenance at the Hotel when he wasn't 'in the bag,' as people around the building would say.

I am sure that Joe Mescall, feeling sorry for my mother, at that point abandoned by my father and in financial straits, offered me work so that I could help at home.

Doctors were the best tippers at the coat check. They made their money from the employed steelworkers' families needing medical care. Once a month, eighty of them settled in for dinner, drinks and cards on a weekend night. This might mean twenty dollars in tips, mostly in quarters for me. That was a lot of money for a boy working from 6:30 p.m. - 1:00 a.m.

I saved the quarters in a brown paper bag, running home in the dark, along Ridge Road, down Electric Avenue and making a right turn onto 29 Apple Street, hoping, with my incredible speed, to ward off late-night thieves who, on roller skates with a fetish for quarters, I was sure were following me.

I didn't know what I would do with my stash, but it wasn't long before I found out. In 1951, my mother wanted me to go to Bishop Timon High School Annex for freshmen in Lackawanna. By then only four of us lived at home: my mother, my sister Susan, four years younger than I, and Beatrice, ten years younger.

In fact, my parents had a shouting match the night I graduated from eighth grade at Benjamin Franklin Elementary School. I have no idea what the details of the quarrel might have been. My father gave me a white plastic Sylvania radio that sat on the kitchen sink for years. After he gave it to me, he slammed the door and walked out. From that night on, Mother's waitressing tips supported us.

The year I entered high school, 1951, Lackawanna was a mill town in every sense of that word. The city, its workers and businesses, experienced this economic rollercoaster for 50 years, but this gets ahead of my story. A mill town experienced growth and good times when the plant was at full production. When Bethlehem and its partners went on strike or suffered a 'lay-off', Lackawanna went into a funk that meant 'red ink' for workers and shop owners. The city relied almost entirely on Bethlehem's payroll and taxes it paid.

In the midst of this turmoil, I began my first year at Bishop Timon High School Annex, run by the Franciscans. I loved school. In 1951, the tuition at Bishop Timon Annex was $5 per month. Sometimes, we couldn't pay it on time. To augment the money I made checking coats, I cut grass that summer in the Holy Cross Cemetery. The cemetery shimmied up alongside Our Lady of Victory Basilica in Lackawanna.

This opportunity came about because Jim Mullett, my friend, talked to his dad, who ran the maintenance operation at the cemetery and he gave us both jobs. In this way, I had the chance to learn the importance of making money on my own. We zoomed around that quiet ground with lawnmowers, nicking an occasional gravestone along the way. (Jim started Canisius College with me years later. He didn't graduate, instead enlisting in the Navy and dying in an auto accident while on duty.)

I cut around Father Baker's grave for a long time each week. I was hoping for a sign from him, or at least a whisper, about how to live my life, but nothing observable happened. I think that Father Baker nudged my Aunt Jean and Uncle Babe, my mother's brother and sister. They supplemented my funds to pay tuition that year. However, just as quickly as the Franciscans came to Lackawanna, they left and went back to Bishop Timon High School in South Buffalo.

Why did the Franciscans move back to South Buffalo? At the time, the Catholic Diocese of Buffalo, including Lackawanna, was in the midst of a high school building boom. Earlier, church authorities decided to integrate the Timon Annex in Lackawanna into the main building of Bishop Timon High School in South Buffalo. The Franciscans did this in 1952, making way for the new Father Baker High School to commence in the same set of buildings in Lackawanna as the earlier annex had been situated.

The arrival of the new priests, all of them young, except for the principal, Father Dennis Sughrue, C.S.C., began with a flourish. In June of 1952, my Aunt Jean made friends with Father Bill Gartland, who stopped in to the Hotel Lackawanna for dinner. When my aunt told him of my need for work, he talked to his superior, Father Sughrue, who offered me some summer employment before my sophomore year. I would be the phone receptionist, along with polishing floors in the building under renovation to become a school.

All summer long, I answered the phone: "Father

Baker High School, May I help you?" while running a large, swirling electric floor polisher throughout the school when the phone wasn't ringing. This procedure made for many missed calls. When I could hear the ring of the phone, I'd drop the polisher and sprint to the office. This made for ruts in the linoleum and out-of-breath exclamations to callers who likely wondered if there wasn't something funny going on at Father Baker High.

Time passed and I made enough money for tuition. I bought a brown school sweater with gold lettering that signified Father Baker High School colors. I was proud of that sweater. It gave me an identity. My new identity attached itself to a saintly deceased priest, Father Nelson Baker, a Baptist convert to Catholicism. Father Baker, as I noted earlier, founded Our Lady of Victory Basilica, a hospital, girls' high school, orphans' home and other charities on Limestone Hill at the corner of Ridge Road and South Park Avenue in Lackawanna. He died in 1936, the year before I was born.

Father Robert Griffin, C.S.C., my English teacher at Father Baker's, along with Father Bill Gartland, another Holy Cross father, who taught me French, were big influences in my life. Many evenings Jim Mullett and I, at a loss about what to do - homework never cross our minds - would call on Father Griffin in the priests' guest room at Father Baker High School. "Should we work at the plant?" We asked him. He never said 'yes' or never said 'no.' "You'll have to work that out," was his reply.

We would sit and chat with Father Griffin, whom students called "Pear", because he was grossly overweight. He sat in his black soutane and opined about life, to our delight. Father Griffin gave us a view of the wider world talking about politics, literature and art, vistas we hardly knew existed.[23] Griffin went on to make his mark at Notre Dame, doing what he did best, being a kind host and listener, a saintly person, who gave those with little, a great deal.

On the other hand, Father Gartland was not a listener; he was a doer. Gartland had a great interest in baseball. He was from Boston and taught me French with a Boston accent. I usually got 99 percent in his exams. I knew all of the French that Father Gartland knew, which wasn't much. He loved sports and I played baseball, first base. In his eyes, I was golden.

High school was a happy time for me, with sports and work. When I got to college, my French grade was somewhere in the basement. Layton Waters, an erudite professor, taught me French at Canisius College, and I went back to basic French with him to catch up on what I never knew I had missed.

Later, just out of high school, I worked any job I could get at #2 Open Hearth, enabling me to take bigger chances - and, still later, catching new opportunities - in teaching, school administration, government work and more.[24]

In fact, earlier Bethlehem workers can multiply whatever recollections I have. About the ebb and flow of employment at Bethlehem: Men are never ready to be laid off, or let go. Somehow, it seemed unreal that so large an entity as the Lackawanna plant would be dismantled. It is fact, however, and there were signs of trouble years earlier.

Lackawanna Steel Company's Lackawanna plant was antiquated by 1922. That was the year Bethlehem Steel, the second largest steel company in the U.S., purchased Lackawanna Steel for $60 million and modernized it with another 40 million dollars. It was also the year that Eugene Gifford Grace became president of the Corporation at age 39. In the same year, he set up the Loop Course, a management-training program used extensively for the next 50 years and some of whose members I knew.

In the twenties, Bethlehem's idea was to use Buffalo, with an auto industry of its own and access via the Great Lakes to the Midwest's economy, to produce steel plates for automobiles and war materiel for the country, when needed.

You have to keep in mind that the Lackawanna plant was one of many steel - producing plants balanced in a juggling act by the corporation. When times were good, as in the 1930s, Bethlehem's steel was used for the Golden Gate Bridge, the George Washington Bridge, Rockefeller Center, the Waldorf-Astoria, Chicago's Merchandise Mart and the U.S. Supreme Court; the company was on a roll. Bethlehem always tried to minimize the role of unions, even to the point of establishing a company union in 1938 that the court disbanded as an unfair labor practice.

By 1941, violent strikes hit the company's Bethlehem, PA plant. The company was in no mood to capitulate to labor and it pushed back. Bethlehem had 170,000 employees at the start of World War II. The following year, the company employed 283,000, its highest number of workers.

By 1957, when I was two years at the plant, Eugene Grace had died and Arthur Homer became president. Edward F. Martin, earlier a superintendent at the Lackawanna plant, succeeded him seven years later. Lackawanna Mayor Walter Paryz died an early death that same year, and Mayor John C. Ogarek took his place. (My father said the Irish elected Ogarek because they thought he was one of them, mistaking his name for O'Garek.) Steel production fell to a three-year-low in that same year, with only 21 of 35 open-hearth furnaces running. Layoffs were moderate because the plant ran on a four day a week schedule.[25]

During those years, I used to bring open-hearth production charts into Ed Martin's office at the Old North Office Building next to #1 Gate. Something that seemed sheer nuttiness to me was the white rug in Mr. Martin's office. What did I know? I felt guilty about getting the rugs dirty with my filthy steelworker's boots every time I entered.

However, nobody in the office ever said anything about my defilement. They just took the production sheets from me, didn't look up and said, "Good bye."

Chapter 3: Working at #2 Open Hearth

Reader, with your permission, go back two years to 1955, when I got some good news as an anxious high school senior at Father Baker High. Canisius College sent me a letter of acceptance for the September 1955 term as a pre-med major.

I chose Canisius because I was impressed with a Jesuit priest I had met, Father Justin Hanley. He looked like Randolph Scott, the movie star. We sat together at a dinner that the college sponsored for high school yearbook editors in the fall of 1954. I attended the dinner at the Hotel Statler in Buffalo, representing Father Baker High, even though I had no money for school. Attending college cost hundreds of dollars a semester and I didn't have a job.

In a panic, because we had no money for me to enroll, my mother called a friend of the family, Norm Fennie. Fennie was then Assistant Superintendent of #2 Open Hearth at Bethlehem Steel's Lackawanna plant. He got me a job as a laborer. I was glad for the chance, although at that point I never considered it to be my life's work.

At that time, almost anybody could get a job at the plant, because the plant needed laborers in every department. Placement in a particular place like the open hearth, however, required some "pull." I knew a few people who worked at #2 Open Hearth: school friends Kevin Fennie, Norm's nephew and his brother Jim's son, and Bill Gavin and his father, Tom, who were third helpers on the furnaces. They had little influence. Fennie was the key and he unlocked the #1 Gate door of the plant for me.

"Just don't get killed, kid," Fennie told me when I went to his office wearing a white helmet, indicating a fledgling worker. "Pick up a broom and sweep where it's safe. I don't want to tell your mother that you got knocked off in here. And don't let me see you standing around, God damn it. Stay busy, even at 3:00 a.m."

That was the advice Norm Fennie gave me in June 1955. I learned what he said wasn't bad advice for life.

I didn't realize that I'd be working in the open hearth for the next eight years, well beyond my college graduation and after starting a teaching career at Lafayette and Grover Cleveland High Schools on the west side of Buffalo, New York. I never stood around, picking up a broom to stay busy if I had nothing else to do.

The furnaces threw off an eerie, hot, orange, 2800 degree Fahrenheit light into the darkness that engulfed the shop. If you were a first or second helper, peering into the furnace to check the consistency of the 'bath', or bubbling heat, you held an elbow up in front of your face, or a shovel, to shield you from the blast of hot air shooting out the wicket hole of the door.

Norm Fennie, my mother and father's friend, was a compulsive character as he walked up and down in front of the furnaces at #2 Open Hearth. He was small and neat in a brown suit, vest and pork pie hat, constantly moving the fingers of both his hands as he walked and talked, as if he was silently typing in the air.

He graduated from Canisius College in the early 40s with his twin brother, Roy. Both worked in steel mills in California as well as Buffalo. Norm, I am told, later left Bethlehem in the 1970s under a cloud. I am not sure why this may be so, but I am not surprised.

The open hearths were 'old' when I began in 1955. #2 Open Hearth had first begun construction in 1912, with two 200-ton tilting models of Bessemer furnaces. Of course, I didn't know this as a young man. I was lucky to stumble in and out of the plant at the beginning and close of shift work, with other things on my mind.

Here is some background: #2 Shop had its first furnace 'tap out' on 29 May 1913, a month after my mother was born. It had huge, 150-250 ton furnaces built and remodeled over time whose numbers ran from #21 to #30, the latter on the north end of the building. I spent a good part of my life at the north end over eight years at the plant as part of the bull gang, supplying stock to the furnaces.

Two other open-hearth complexes, #1 Open Hearth, was the first built in 1903, and #3 Open Hearth, the last of the three steel producing facilities constructed in Lackawanna, was completed in 1929. These additions comported with Bethlehem's view of what it needed to deal with overall open-hearth steel production for the company. Years later, in 1964, basic oxygen furnaces began to replace the open hearth, or Siemens-Martin process of making steel. Why? They were able to knock back the time to produce a 200-ton heat of steel from nine - ten hours to four hours.[26]

Perhaps you can sense my nervousness when I arrived at # 1 Gate at the Lackawanna Plant on my first day of work in June 1955. I was dumbfounded. I had just stepped off the bus from Ridge Road down to Bethlehem in the dark, about 6:15 a.m. I carried a small, brown paper bag with a sandwich I made, some work clothes in a bundle and a towel. After I showed my badge to Bethlehem security at the gate, I wasn't sure where to go. A helpful plant cop said, "Just walk straight ahead, kid."

"Straight ahead?" In front of me moved huge narrow gauge engines, pushing heats of steel on flatbed cars that interrupted our foot traffic. I stood completely still, confounded by the sight. The steel ingots were lighted up like huge orange popsicles in the dark, and they burnt your face as you stopped to look at them.

The heat near the steel ingots was intense. If you were one of the few driving a car inside the plant, the blistering heat of the stripped ingots, perhaps over

2000 degrees Fahrenheit, could peel the paint off your car. Danger was everywhere, yet men who were used to the environment walked past me as nonchalantly as if they were out for a Sunday walk in the park.

I finally found my way to #2 Open Hearth labor shanty, where the foreman, Mike Dolan, introduced himself to me. Dolan was a kindly Irishman, mid-30s, agreeable and knowledgeable about all elements of his work, "the prince of the open hearth", as Eddie Seifert, a second helper, called him. Seifert started work at Bethlehem a few days after Dolan, in January 1952. From time to time, when Dolan was nervous, he bit his fingernails. There was nothing left to them but the quick.

Mike tossed me the white helmet, (I caught it), indicating that I was a new employee. He also had some goggles, gloves, and a note to the stores department for me to get a pair of steel-toed work shoes,

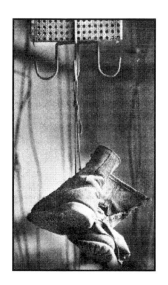

LOCKERS AT BETHLEHEM THAT DESCENDED FROM THE CEILING IN WASHROOM.

PHOTO: THE MORNING CALL

charged to my payroll account.

Dolan took me to the locker room, pulled down a vacant locker on chains from the ceiling, and told me to put on open-hearth garb: a helmet, safety glasses, and work-shoes with steel toes, giving me a heavy dark blue wool Bethlehem jacket and gloves.

Back at the labor shanty Dolan gave me my first assignment, saying, "Sweep up on the tracks from the scrap yards. Watch out for moving 'buggies' and scrap coming into the open hearth to be charged."

The furnaces were one flight up, on the floor of the Open Hearth. I climbed the steps. My eyes widened as I entered the open hearth itself. It was like Dante's inferno: dark, with flashing sheets of light bursting from the furnaces, burning at 3000 degrees Fahrenheit inside.

Mechanical doors, five to each furnace (seven on #'s 21 & 22 furnaces), raised open at the first helper's direction to enable charging machines that dumped pans of scrap metal, like one's hand turning over, each weighing 3000 - 6000 pounds, depending upon what scrap was in them, into the furnace during its 'charging' phase.

Overhead, cranes carried heavy cargo like bricks, pallets of lead bars, huge metal boxes of manganese and low-carbon chrome, phosphorus, dolomite and spar, which would be dumped on the floor of the open hearth, or, into bins, for furnace use. Norm Fennie wasn't kidding; a guy could get killed in this place.

In retrospect, I am amazed to realize how little things had changed from the earlier days of steelmaking. In the summer of 1919, a young lieutenant, Charles R. Walker, recently discharged from the army, "...bought some second-hand clothes and went to work on an open-hearth furnace near Pittsburgh to learn the steel business."[27]

Walker's diary records 36 years earlier the same experiences that I had when beginning open-hearth work. To begin with, there was his amazement at the floor of the shop, where the top portions of the furnaces were located.

Walker wrote, "I was first conscious of the blaring mouths of the furnaces. There were five of them, and men with shovels in line, marching within a yard, hurling white gravel down red throats. Two of the men were stripped, and their backs were shiny in the red flare....Some one yelled, "Watch yourself!" and I looked up, with some horror, to note half the mill moving slowly but resolutely onward, bent on my annihilation. I was mistaken. It was the charging-machine, rattling and grinding past furnace No. 7."

I would not change a word of Walker's description on my own first day of work.

Of course, mechanical, electrical and structural changes were made over the years, but they would be the equivalent of replacing parts of a watch, without altering its basic design.

Soon, thanks to Mike Dolan, I began working along side a group of college guys, Ken Seifert, the younger brother of Ed, Jim McLaughlin, and Bill Orrange. Dolan added a couple of teachers to our crew, Jack Foster and Don Miller. Members of the bull gang might start the day on a 7 to 3 shift by carrying 50 pound, 10 foot long clay-baked thermocouples to the each of the furnaces, from #21 - #30. Of course, we worked nights, 11 - 7 and sometimes doubled up, working 16 hours one or both days on weekends, if needed. It was big money at time and a half or sometimes, on a holiday, double time.

Thermocouples, poked through the center of the doors of the furnace by the first helper, measured temperature in the furnace 'bath' of molten steel, usually up around 2800 F. These temperatures were one index of determining the readiness of the steel heat to be tapped at the back of the furnace.

In addition, we stocked the bins on the floor of the furnaces with 100-pound bags of aluminum pellets, manganese, phosphorus, low carbon chrome, sulphur, nickel bars, molybdenum, titanium, sulphur and other ingredients required for particular grades of steel.

100-pound paper bags of sulphur when used for steel-making sent everybody to the railings of the building, gasping for air. Sulphur that catches fire shuts the respiratory system down, making it hard to breathe. If sulphur caught fire in its storage area, it was tough to put out, burning with an almost secretive, gagging blue flame.

These various bull gang chores made it a rigorous job physically, but enjoyable as long as you were young and in shape. Occasionally, as we developed seniority, we were able to take turns as third and second helpers on the furnaces. Third helpers' jobs involved shoveling dolomite and spar into the furnaces to reconfigure the 'breasts' of the doors. The dolomite also shored up the tap-hole area in the back of the furnace after a heat had been tapped.

Second helpers directed the 'spoon' at the doors of the furnace for the 'gun', a large conveyor belted machine with dolomite poured in at the top by a crane and directed by the first helper or occasionally, the third helpers to make up the back wall. You had to make sure as a third helper that your shovels of fluorspar landed on top of the slag to get rid of it. Otherwise, as Charles R. Walker wrote earlier, "Spar eats the dolomite as mice eat cheese."[28]

Second helpers made up spouts after successfully tapping the furnaces. The most important part of spout-making for second helpers was to insure that there was a 'good joint' made, that is, one that had bricks and other materials supporting it firmly, so that steel did not insinuate itself between the furnace and the ladle when the furnace tapped out, spilling on the pit-side floor. These jobs paid more per hour. If you screwed up, you got time off.

From time to time, I would see Norm Fennie's older brother, Jimmy, a close family friend, working as an inspector in the Open Hearths. Jim, an accountant by trade, worked at the plant, I suppose, to make extra money for the family. He took tests before each heat was poured to measure appropriate manganese, phosphorus, sulphur and carbon and other chemical levels.

As Walker wrote about these tests in 1917, "The first-helper will take a spoon about the size of your hand and scoop up some of the soup, but not to taste. He pours it into a mould, and when the little ingot is cool, breaks it with a sledge. Everyone on the furnace, barring myself, looks at the broken metal and gives a wise smile. ... They know by the grain if she has too much carbon or needs more, or is ready to tap or isn't. With too much carbon, she'll need a "jigger," which is a few more tons of hot metal, to thin her out."[29]

This process didn't change much over the next thirty-five years. The same moulds were used, sledged, and carbon checked in the mid-50s. Somewhat later, a pneumatic tube was used to send a 'test', via vacuum to a lab situated elsewhere in the plant, for analysis. In a sense, the use of the mould to take a test to see if the steel was ready to pour was a paradigm for the entire steel process changing insufficiently to keep up with progress in other parts of the world.

Open hearth superintendent Norm Fennie was a fascinating character to me. He seemed to make his entire life the steel plant. At that point, I was too young to realize how complicated human beings can be. I didn't know - nor do I know now - Fennie's reasons for being obsessed with the steel plant.

Earlier, however, as an example of his overheated dedication, he rang up one night on the 11 p.m. - 7 a.m. shift, asking for me after talking to the melter.

It was 3 a.m., and what did he ask? "How's my Open Hearth?" Think about it. What kind of a life was he living to interrupt his sleep and ask about his open hearth, as if it were a lover?

In fact, I did think about it. Fennie became the inspiration for a story I wrote that highlighted his incredible drive to produce record 'heats' at No. 2 Open Hearth. I include the story here as it gives a flavor of what work at Bethlehem's Lackawanna open hearths was like some 50 years ago.

The story represents what I thought was an archetypal obsession with production and success among vying superintendents and melters at the three open-hearth facilities in the Lackawanna plant.

****

"The next page: Feeling the heat at the No. 2 Open Hearth

A story of a steel-driven man" from the Pittsburgh-Post Gazette

Sunday, March 08, 2009.

In 1900, Buffalo was a leading port on Lake Erie, a gateway to the West. It manufactured flour and was a huge railroad hub. Buffalo developed into a major city because of hydroelectric power and the growth of heavy industry, represented by Bethlehem Steel, Hanna Furnace and automakers. Buffalo was a melting pot of more than 60 nationalities living and occasionally fighting, as they worked side by side.

In the last 100 years, a major contributor to Buffalo's prosperity, Bethlehem Steel, has gone from a major industry to a non-entity. By 1990, The Washington Post marked the demise of Bethlehem in Lackawanna, N.Y. "This is the city that big steel built and that big steel brought down," the story began.

I was interviewed for the article: " 'It was a vital, active place,' said Michael D. Langan, who worked in the Lackawanna plant for eight years while he was going to college and later when he started a teaching career in Buffalo. 'But it doesn't exist anymore.' "

Over the past 20 years or so, I have changed my mind about Bethlehem Steel's demise. We make too little of what exists in one's memory. Bethlehem is alive in imagination, as real as it was in 1955.

The value of memory is that it can tell the story of a living, breathing, steel-making life pulsing with energy. It remains real, even though it existed before many adults today shook a rattle.

This is a story about the all-consuming nature of work at the plant, shift work that, for some, blotted out family life, weekend golf, even a drink after work for those who gave their lives to steel and Bethlehem. It also tells the companion story of men (there were few women there at that time) who relied on the plant for paychecks. The weekly check took care of family expenses: the mortgage, groceries and kids' clothes. Extra money came from overtime to buy Christmas gifts and an extra load of coal in the basement for their winter heat. Now all of this is gone.

Let me tell you a story about how it was, a story about a superintendent of No. 2 Open Hearth at the Bethlehem Plant in Lackawanna in the 1950s.

I have changed identities, but old-timers will recognize personalities — and I hope that many Pittsburghers recognize their history here, too. The determination of one steel-driven man in this story has outlasted the company itself.

Aug. 31, 1959, 7:00 a.m.

"Phelps is on the phone, Norm," said the chief clerk.

"Thanks, Hank. I'll take it in my office." Norm Clark turned the key to his tile-walled office door. His desk stood atop a four-inch pedestal that covered half the room. Norm picked up the phone.

"Morning, Carl."

"Hello, Norm," the general superintendent said. "Listen. Great going on the shop production this month. You're within reach of your own record."

"What do you mean, reach?" asked Norm, cocky, assured.

"We'll break it today. I have 23 furnace lined up to make a 300-ton nickel-chrome-moly heat. You know what these alloy heats are like, Carl. I'll have to really pull for temperature if we're going to get it out in time to break the record."

"What time did it charge back?" Phelps asked with a note of concern.

"4 a.m.," Norm said flatly.

"You can't do it, Norm. You'll burn the roof of the furnace and cost us more than any lousy record is worth."

"I've got it figured out, Carl. We need 2980 degrees Fahrenheit temperature. I'm going to blow the heat down with the oxygen lance at 7:45 a.m. I figure that if we can drop carbon by 25 points in an hour, there'll be a chance."

Phelps became more assertive. "Forget it, Clark. That basic roof furnace melts at 3000 degrees. I don't want a crippled furnace, a quarter-million-dollar loss and 200 men working overtime because of your pig-headedness. Forget it."

Norm Clark didn't say anything for a moment. He was calculating how to reach Phelps.

"Be reasonable, Carl. Tomorrow is the big meeting at the Main Office, One Gate. I'd like nothing better than to throw another record in the mill foremen's faces. It would be good for both of us."

Carl's voice became testy. "I said, 'No,' Norm. Forget about the record. There are more important things."

"He's too damned conservative," Norm thought, hanging up on Carl.

Norm shouted out to his clerk, Hank: "Check the air filtration reports on 28 and 30 furnaces. I want a complete rundown on the fantail brickwork on 24 furnace for the past five years," he said.

Norm got up from his desk and walked to the window overlooking the scrap yard. He was a small man in stature. But when you heard him bellow at one of the operators of the huge overhead cranes on the furnace floor, he wasn't small any more.

Somehow, after you worked with him for a while, he seemed to grow before your eyes. His mastery of steelmaking made him seem tall and angular as the sprawling Open Hearth itself.

Norm Clark knew he would succeed. He put himself through Canisius College in the early 1940s by working the 11-to-7 shift each night. He built his reputation, first as a labor foreman, then as a turn foreman, then as a melter and finally, as an assistant superintendent. It was quite a shock to him when his mentor, old McSweeney, died of a heart attack on the job. But he jumped at the chance to succeed, and, when he was chosen over a number of younger, better educated engineers, he was pleased.

"Phelps is getting old," Norm thought. Another year and he would retire. "Who'd get Phelps' job?" He, DeMatteo and York were in line for it. How would a decision be made? Relative merits, that's how. Here was his chance to show who was the best man.

"Hank, get Lafferty the melter on the phone at 23 furnace. Tell him I want to see him in my office, now!"

"OK, Norm," Hank said mechanically. The day's

routine might have been a challenge to some; for most, it was monotonous. Hank put himself in this latter category. Work was a place to go to make a buck to buy a beer, nothing more.

Lafferty was in Norm's office in three minutes. He was nervous, red-faced and out of breath.

"You probably want to know why I made that 'off-heat' yesterday, right, Norm?"

"Lafferty," Norm Clark said in his best authoritative style, eyes peering over his black-banded, half-glasses: "In just two minutes I want you to drop the oxygen lance into 23 furnace. Run 50,000 cubic feet of oxygen for one hour into that bath of steel. I want a pull of 2980 degrees F by 8:15 this morning."

Norm continued, "I'll be out to see the heat tap. Line up the pit foreman to set two bifurcated spouts in back of the furnace in case anything goes wrong with the tap. Make a mistake and I'll put you back third-helping until you can't remember what a good tonnage check looks like."

"Whatever you say, Norm." Lafferty swallowed hard, for he knew that Norm was pushing the furnace to its physical limit. He knew better than to argue.

"Do you need it that hot in such a short time?" Lafferty asked.

Norm looked down from his platform.

"Yes. Now don't waste any more of my time."

It was about 8:00 a.m. when Carl Phelps began

his tour of the three open hearths that were his responsibility.

His practice was always to begin at No. 1 Open Hearth and to proceed until he reached Norm's No. 2 Shop before lunch. That morning, however, Norm's tone had disturbed him. He began his tour at Norm's shop.

As he climbed the double landing to the floor of No. 2 Open Hearth, he turned over in his mind the rapidity and assurance that Norm possessed in making decisions. A valuable asset, he thought, but not without the liability of being wrong occasionally. He had never known Norm to be wrong when it came to big decisions, though. However, this record business was becoming a fetish with him. It could spoil his good judgment in time.

With his expert eye in furnace matters, Phelps could see that there was unusual activity in front of No. 23 furnace. Men were scurrying about in the half darkness of the shop, like ants on a dark cellar floor.

"What's going on, Lafferty?" asked Phelps in the tone of a concerned overseer.

"Norm wants to heat her up in a hurry, Mr. Phelps. He'll be down in a few minutes. He says it's important that we tap No. 23 by 8:15 a.m."

"I see," said Phelps. He turned sternly cold. Lafferty watched him walk stiffly into the observer's shanty at No. 24 furnace. Carl Phelps dialed No. 588, the main office of the general manager of Bethlehem Steel's Lackawanna Plant.

"Let me speak to Mr. White, please," said Phelps.

"Cy, this is Carl Phelps calling from No. 2 Open Hearth. Sorry to bother you, but Norm Clark has gone against my orders on furnace production. It looks as if No. 23 furnace is going to burn down to its rider arches."

White spoke unhesitatingly. "I'll be right over."

As Phelps left the observer's shanty, he met and joined Norm Clark in his usual, rapid gait. Norm always walked quickly, hands moving nervously, fingers flicking into space as if it were a typewriter expressing his unspoken thoughts.

"I've called Cy White, Norm," Phelps said. "He's on his way over."

"OK with me," Norm said. He appeared unconcerned.

"This could mean your job, Norm. You forced me to do this."

But it was Carl Phelps who began to unravel. Could Norm be pushing this thing to prove himself a better man than his general superintendent?

Did Norm plan it? Had he been maneuvered?

They were in front of No. 23 furnace.

Norm spoke rapidly to Lafferty. He eyed the key brick of the basic roof of the furnace. Through dark glasses, he observed stalactites of silica beginning to form on the brick - the initial step in roof damage.

"How much temperature you got, Lafferty?"

"2975, Norm."

"When did you take it?"

"Five minutes ago, in three-door, Norm."

"Pull the oxygen lance up and dig out the heat. It's ready."

Cy White, the plant superintendent, a man in his mid-50s, Brooks Brothers-suited and Ivy League-trained, heard the last command as he came within earshot.

"Morning, Mr. White," Norm said inattentively, as he passed him in the way behind the furnace. "We've got a record here. Stick around."

"See here, Clark, I ..."

Norm Clark was gone. The furnace was as big as half a football field.

The second helpers had a rough time digging out the heat. They used air, finally grabbing an oxygen torch devised to blast the steel out. Ten minutes went by. The wailing siren warned men on the pit side of the furnace of impending danger.

Norm knew that the longer a "flat" heat of steel sits in a furnace, the greater danger of roof damage. Norm strode down the platform behind the furnace and grabbed the oxygen lance out of the second helper's hand. He plunged the lance into the soft clay plug that was at the heart of the tap hole. Behind it lay

250 tons of alloy steel. Working feverishly, Norm manhandled the rod until its hot end burned away every impediment to the onrush of captive steel.

Out with a flash into the darkness came the steel, bright as the Fourth of July!

It was a good heat. Its glow as it went into the ladle reflected the mood of three men.

Carl Phelps left more quietly and quickly than he came. He shielded his face from the light that was to cast a shadow on his final year as general superintendent.

Cy White was impressed. "Nice heat, Norm," White said with a bravado that his voice was unaccustomed to carrying. He was clearly impressed with Norm Clark.

Norm Clark was not listening. He was mesmerized by the glow of the steel as it hit the ladle below.

Today, Carl Phelps, Cy White and Norm Clark have punched out and are working the 11-to-7 shift somewhere in eternity.

Bethlehem Steel is almost gone. What remains of it is the glint of recognition in old men's eyes who remember.

"Nice heat, Norm."[30]

✶✶✶✶✶✶✶✶✶✶✶✶✶✶✶✶✶✶✶

Chapter 4: Boilermakers Before Breakfast

For a number of years I worked in the bull gang with college students, people I mentioned briefly earlier: Jim McLaughlin, whose father was a melter in the open hearths, Bill Orrange, a Latin major at Canisius, and Ken Seifert, an education major at Buffalo State. For all of us, the idea of 'promise' kept us going, I think. When you are young you may not always think of the future, but you want to have that feeling that, if you work hard, you can get somewhere.

A couple of 'older' guys, still in their 20s, Jack Foster and Don Miller, were teachers of history and shop, respectively, working extra hours to make more money for their families. Jack and Don instilled this feeling of promise to the younger members of the bull gang. They were professional, respectful and hard working. Together, we made a good team. The work never ended but it was something to do if you were young and needed the money.

Plenty of men from the Buffalo area populated bull gangs at Bethlehem in those years. Their purpose was the same: hard, introductory work in the plant done by workers who wanted a job, and maybe a career in steelmaking.

When I started out in the 'bull gang' at #2 Open Hearth in 1955, we had plenty of jobs given to us by the labor foreman. The bull gang leader, something I eventually worked into, coordinated and delivered the supplies needed. We directed supplies lifted by crane from the north and south end of the shop. From those entry points, they were lifted up about 60 feet onto the floor of the open hearth and offloaded for use on the furnaces, as well as moved to the pit-side of the open hearth. There supplies like brick were used to re-line ladles, slurry molds, and other needs requested by the pit foreman.

Bull gang workers lifted 100-pound burlap bags of aluminum pellets, heaved 75-pound bars of nickel and carried thermocouples to furnaces for heat testing. The bull gang leader would contact the bulldozer operator and tell him to load huge boxes of coal or spar, placing cans of molybdenum onto a pallet and raised with cable slings by an overhead crane. He would also coordinate with the overhead crane operators on the floor of the open hearth, letting them know of impending, required lifts to the second story 'floor' of the open hearth.

The bull gang had more work than it could finish. Add a lift truck and a pay loader, a small bulldozer, used for scooping up other materials - stock, such as low carbon chrome, manganese and phosphorus for the furnaces, and you get an idea of the day's work confronting young steelworkers.

Being paid was the end of the rainbow each

week. Each Friday morning at 7 a.m., the entire shift of workers would line up on the stairwell landing just below the superintendent's office on the 2nd floor. Each employee showed his badge to Henry Woyshner, the open-hearth clerk, who would promptly give out the weekly checks.

"532 1449, Henry", I'd say.

"Here's your check, Mike. Remember: Straight home", Woyshner would say, knowing that almost

A Bethlehem Steel ID enabling the bearer to enter the Lackawanna plant. Langan's open hearth number, "BC 1451" was changed in later years to badge number "532 1449" when the company made an adjustment in how it identified workers.

nobody ever went straight home. Many went out to drink.

There was a potential problem: how do you cash checks at that time of the morning? Banks weren't open. There was one way. You could stop at the Liberty Restaurant on the corner of Ridge Road, just up from #1 Gate.

If you ordered a bottle of beer and a shot of whiskey - a 'boilermaker before breakfast' - you got your check cashed, at the Liberty, no charge. This was a simple and efficient way to get money when you needed it. However, it was an embarrassment to smell of liquor if you were a college student taking the bus to class. People on the bus made their silent, opprobrious judgments about your moral state as they looked at you.

I often wondered over the years, what happened to these young men, old men now. I knew a bit about some of them. Dr. Jack Foster for example, took a doctorate in history from Ball State University in Indiana. He became a professor of history at Southern Connecticut State University in New Haven, CT.

When I first knew him at the plant, Jack was out of the army and teaching history in Orchard Park, NY and coaching track. Bethlehem gave him the chance to be even busier in a young life, with some money earned that put him on track to continue his graduate education. Jack was in our wedding in 1959.

Fifty years later, Jack at age 80 and I at age 73,

found that we lived within miles of each other in Naples, FL. In all those years, we never spoke until I talked to Jack on the phone in February of 2010 and followed up with a get-re-acquainted lunch with him and his wife, Liz, in April at the Brio Restaurant in the Waterside Mall.

Jack talked about the jobs we did in the bull gang, getting supplies for the furnaces up from the north end of #2 Shop with a crane, as well as making special heats. His favorite job, he told me, was keeping the charts on the open-hearth furnaces up-to-date. Every furnace was required to keep accurate chartings of fuel and temperature over 24 hours.

I knew a bit more about Dr. Kenneth R. Seifert,

JOANNE ERNST AND MICHAEL D. LANGAN, MARRIED JUNE 20, 1959. JOANNE'S SISTER, LUCILE HEALY, APPEARS AT THE TOP LEFT AND SUSAN LANGAN (DECEASED), MIKE'S SISTER, APPEARS LOWER LEFT. ON THE RIGHT ARE ANGELO MASSARO, MIKE'S BEST MAN, AND MIKE DOLAN AND JACK FOSTER IN DESCENDING ORDER, OPEN HEARTH FRIENDS.

PHOTO: DAVID BORCHARD

who received a doctorate from Cornell University in school administration and held a number of principal and superintendent positions across the country before settling for many years in Andover, MA, as superintendent of schools there, and retiring in 1990, doing consulting work and interim superintendent jobs until 2006. He then started a radio show and wrote for newspapers.

I spoke to Ken a few times by phone over the years. Seifert has a wicked sense of humor and is a fine writer. I think that his work at Bethlehem gave him a sympathy for how tough life could be for older workers there. Seifert was an intellectual at an early age, although he may never accept that term. By 'intellectual', I meant that he analyzed people and events within Bethlehem with rigor.

If a worker wasn't doing his job and Seifert was in charge, he chewed the guy out. He was insightful and sharp; not somebody to mess with. He still is a tough character, a long-ago winner of the bantamweight Golden Gloves in his teenage years.

In early 2010, Seifert summarized his career this way to me in an e-mail. "I taught school in Germany for a couple of years. I married Norma, a gal from Corning, NY. I became an elementary principal at 26. I took a doctorate from Cornell. I became Assistant Superintendent of Clark County, Nevada schools at 31. I was Supcrintendent of Schools in Andover at 34, retired at 56. I have consulted for 10 years and spend time fly-fishing, gardening and traveling with my wife of fifty years. I taught at some good universities along the way. I have four children, five and one half grandchildren."

Ken continued, "I write a weekly column for the local newspaper for fun. Life could not be better and I have been very fortunate to have had seventy-five meaningful and full years. I don't know why I have been so lucky. I am still the same kid from South Buffalo with a level of sophistication given to me from Norma and Cornell."

Ken once told me that he thought the open-hearth fraternity was a real brotherhood. He wrote, "The work force ages spanned decades on each shift, but they had a lot in common: The battle with the heat and heavy labor. There was a necessity to work together to get the heat out and into the ladle. Real steel men knew how the pieces fit."

Seifert continued, "It was a day in heaven and hell that got into your blood. As guys showered up after a shift and new guys came in, it was like WW I troops coming and going to the front. The expressions were similar. If you had a rough day, you'd be dragging out the gate. If you had a good day, you'd be happy go lucky, going out."

He finished by writing, "It was ... an experience that demanded more effort than the average job and we shared that environment at Bethlehem with a United Nations' group who had a great deal in common. In the end we were tapped out but what a heat we made."

Ken was cut from the same rough cloth as his

older brother, Eddie Seifert, who also worked in open-hearth, rising through the ranks and working in the pulpit of the basic oxygen furnaces (BOF). Eddie, who put nine kids through college, was also one of the union presidents, along with Arthur Sambucci, another stalwart of that era of union-company negotiations and both tough defenders of workers' rights.

Bill Orrange, a classics major at Canisius College when I knew him at the plant, wrote me 55 years later, in 2010, about his recollections at Bethlehem. Bill had a 'can do' attitude at Bethlehem that carried over to his various careers in the military and thereafter. At the plant, if he was given a job, you could count on it to be done.

His description of his own life is a demonstration of those core attributes of honesty, reliability and intelligence that he reinforced while working at the plant.

"Dear Mike," he wrote, "Like you, Two Shop has never left my mind and I remember our time there as an exciting experience to which I always looked forward with a bit of heart pounding anticipation.

The delay in writing is due to apprehension that my memories are not well fleshed out, perhaps inaccurate and more personal than enlightening but here goes. I hope there is something useful in these rather unconnected recollections.

First, getting to work in Lackawanna is a mysterious part of my Buffalo experience. I lived in the Riverside/Black Rock neighborhood. I don't remember reflecting at all at the time about the fact that I took three buses to Canisius High School and two to the College every day in winter. I believe I took just two to and from Lackawanna, but that was often very early in the morning or in the middle of the night. I have a sharp memory of standing in a dark and empty Niagara Square waiting for the bus down Niagara Street and then up Hertel Avenue to East Street where I lived. Interestingly, the fact that it was often very cold and snowy is not part of the memory.

I don't recall just how I got the job at Bethlehem Steel. I always needed a job to get through college and was constantly searching. I'm quite sure I got the job through Steve Niziol, whose daughter, Stephanie, I was dating. I don't recall whether Steve was a Foreman or a Melter. [Steve was a turn foreman.] It was nice of him to do that for me. He was a quiet man who I did not often see while dating or (later) at the plant. I think Stephanie must have set that up for me.

For years, a favored memento was stored in a footlocker in the home where I grew up. I had long since departed from Buffalo, first to the USMC and then LA. That was my Bethlehem Steel hard hat with the name "Papers" written on it by either Jack Foster or Don Miller, as I recall. When my mother moved to an apartment, I was too stupid to arrange to get hold of the footlocker and it was tossed or given away.

The nickname referred to the fact that I was chilling out (hiding out?) and reading a newspaper in that little room where the labor gang gathered (or maybe it was the ladle liners' shanty.) The plant superintendent (was it Norm Fennie?) walked in and asked what I was doing. What could I say except "reading the paper". Of course, I got booted out and my response was memorialized on my hard hat. "Papers" became my nickname.

I remember sitting in that labor gang room around the salamander — a 50-gallon drum, glowing red from a gas flame piped inside. I always enjoyed eating my packed lunch there, engaged in lively and salty banter, and trading insults. I still like packing the kind of sandwiches I preferred then. Things like fried baloney or olive loaf and a American cheese, grilled. I distinctly recall, before the start of the shift, stopping at the commissary and getting a pint milk bottle with coffee, milk and sugar added. The bottle was scalding hot and had to be handled with gloves on. It was ready to drink a couple of hours later for the lunch break. In memory that was the most delightful coffee I've ever tasted.

Another lunch memory comes to mind. While I don't think there was any formal segregation in the plant, jobs and work areas seemed to form around cliques. The slurry gang was all black, as I recall. From time to time when they were shorthanded one of us would go there to work a shift. Those assignments may have lifted our pay above the labor gang level — is that right? I remember sitting at lunch with the slurry gang. The room was always filled with loud, animated jiving and laughing. It was as though the conversation was in a foreign language. I could not understand a word that was said.

I think there was at least one black first helper, a good-paying job. I also remember that Henry Brimm, a pretty good middleweight who once tied Sugar Ray Robinson, had a job to himself. (Which reminds me: didn't Ken Seifert box, at least as an amateur?)

On the subject of pay, one very fond memory was working the holidays. The regular union workers wanted to be off over the holidays and welcomed us to take over the shifts. More than once I worked three straight shifts and earned a week's pay in one 24-hour period (one shift at regular pay and two at double time — or was it two at time-and-a-half and one at double time?) It was easy to do. I even enjoyed it. There was a relaxed, collegial work atmosphere. The shift foreman assigned a job. When it was finished he said, "go find a place to sack out. Just let me know where to find you".

As for pay, I think we got about $5/hour in the labor gang — no? The pay was certainly far more than a college student could make in any other part-time job. I think foremen and melters earned great money — was it as much as $40k/year, as I recall? In the 50s, that was big money indeed.

I remember, of course, the jobs — shoveling dolomite in a bucket-brigade-style circle to line the walls of an open-hearth furnace, managing the oxygen hose behind a second helper when the furnace was being tapped and preparing special heats. Being nearby for the furnace tapping was a terrific experience, huddled in a wool coat and goggles. You could never know how the furnace would blow. Sometimes, the molten steel would begin running in a benign incandescent stream and other times it was an explosion like a rocket launch.

I can't quite picture the set up for dumping special heats into the charging pans, but I do remember that heats including chromium and manganese could provide a spectacle. As I recall the stock was dumped into a chute. Chrome and manganese are very flinty and strike off sparks. The chute (or whatever) often contained collected dust. You dumped [the wheelbarrow] at arms' length and often were treated to an explosive backfire when a spark ignited the dust. On the subject of stock, I recall being fairly well coated with silicon inside and out. I could blow my nose after a shift and see the shiny metallic material. It somewhat surprises me that I know of no ill effects from this or other environmental hazards — like the deafening noise that filled the plant.

As I remember it there were three serious accidents on shifts I was working. One was fatal for sure. I think you were close to that one — an electrician was walking next to narrow gauge flat cars. As the locomotive bumped the line of cars an iron box that was not properly seated slipped off one of the cars and pinned the poor guy against a sharp iron railing. I can still hear the brief startled cry. It makes me shudder as does the incredible bad luck of his being in just that place at the fatal instant. I remember that everyone around me looked up for an instant and then acted as though nothing happened. No one talked about it.

I'm not sure if the other accidents were fatal although they were certainly serious. I recall that a guy who worked in the scrap yard was struck by a large crane magnet. The job was to stand in a gondola car using a hook to straighten and clear scrap metal lifted by the magnet.

I think we got that job from time to time — no? The cardinal rule was to make sure that the crane operator could see you at all times. Somehow, that broke down and the magnet struck him. In the other case, a guy who worked in the mixer area was scalded when a spill occurred or maybe there was an explosion due to an air bubble in the mixer. I think that happened from time to time.

I don't want to sound like a glutton but when I think of Buffalo, I think of the food I liked there. One of the PhD candidates on our Syria excavation team is from Buffalo (attending Boston University). She and I have challenged our Italian colleagues who are always bragging about the cuisine in Italy. Few things can beat beef on weck, kielbasa or German potato salad. I remember being at one or more parties in Mike Dolan's basement (I think). There was a boiling tub of cooking kielbasa to fish out and eat on a bun, with beer of course. Yummm!"

Bill Orrange continued his recollections, fleshing out his life after leaving school and Bethlehem this way.

"After three years on active duty with USMC, I followed a buddy to graduate school at UCLA in Classics. After about a year and a half it was clear that I was no great scholar and my money was running out. I had been working in the Engineering and Math Sciences Library, often doing literature searches for Aerospace clients. When I mentioned my impending poverty, a group from Rocketdyne said "come with us" to do promotional writing and PR. In those days, the Space Program had tons of money and jobs were plentiful.

That launched me on a career doing PR and promotion for high tech firms. In 1984, a partner and I started our own firm in Palo Alto. I have lived in California the entire period except for two years in the mid-60s working for IBM in White Plains, NY. Although I based my business in Palo Alto, we maintained our Los Angeles home in Pacific Palisades and I split my time.

I continued in the Marine Corps Reserve for a number of years and met my wife Susan through her sister who was the fiancé of a fellow officer. We were married in 1964 and have two daughters and two granddaughters — all living close by.

Susan (now retired) worked for a number of years as admin assistant to the head of Cardiology at the VA/UCLA hospital. She was also the managing editor of a cardiology journal they published. My older daughter, Teresa, works for JP Morgan as a financial manager. She and her boss handle mostly sports celebrity clients. My younger daughter (the mother of our grandchildren), Sharon, is an MD and member of the faculty at USC Medical School in Family Medicine. Before getting her MD from

USC, she earned a Master's in Public Health from Johns Hopkins and worked at CDC."

Bill wound down his interesting e-mail, "As I was looking ahead toward retirement, I had it in mind to return to Latin and Greek Classics for fun. That was my major at Canisius College. When I reviewed the catalog for Continuing Studies at Stanford (near-by in Palo Alto), I discovered archaeology. I took courses from a spellbinding professor and went with his group on a dig at a Roman site in the Alps. After returning to LA for good, I got involved at UCLA with the Mozan/Urkesh team in Syria. I'm very much aware of the misfortune and suffering in the world, much of it close to home and, like you, I ask myself why I've been so lucky. Our days in the steel mill often come to mind. As I remember it, it was exciting and fun," Orrange concluded.

Bethlehem provided another member of our bull gang, Don Miller, "D.T." as we called him, the chance to add money to the coffers of his young family.

Don was a veteran of the Seabees and taught industrial arts in Orchard Park, NY until his retire-ment. He went back to college in the early 1950s. Later, Don was in business, running a driving school in his spare time as well as being an avid sailor. I kept in touch from time to time with Don's family, Gloria, his wife, and his very talented children, now grown to adulthood.

Don had an innate kindness that made people reach out to him. He was a leader among the bull gang members, almost a father figure for some of us.

Don could do just about anything within the plant context; he was so skilled in what we used to call the industrial arts. Bethlehem refined these capacities even more.

In fact, I asked Gloria to put down her recollections about Don and his bull gang days, going to school, working and teaching. Here is what she wrote:

"When we married, three weeks after Don had been discharged from the Navy, a week after my college graduation, and two weeks before Don began undergraduate college, we had no car, no savings, and no other source of income other than my $3,000 year income teaching 8th Grade English and the GI Bill for undergraduate college.

Within two months, Don was hired through his brother's connections with Mike Dolan. We were able to buy a small second hand car, so that Don did not have to continue to take the bus not only to Buff State, but to Bethlehem as well. (I continued to travel to school with one of the other teachers for a small fee.)

I think he continued for 10 years working weekends and a night or two and school holidays and summer vacations at Bethlehem. The plant enabled us to survive financially and to allow Don to complete his education. It seems that once a year or so a check would unexpectedly arrive in the mail for something owed to him! What a delightful surprise! We never questioned it, but eagerly cashed the check.

Don never complained of the hard and dangerous work, but that was Don. In retrospect, I am glad that I was unaware of the danger, for I would have been worried and conflicted. I was amused with his tales of wrestling with the rats, who tried to take his lunch and/or trying to catch some sleep in the wheelbarrow and his stories involving you and Jack. They were even more amusing, when we all got together.

I cannot remember the occasion, but after Don had been at the plant for several years, he introduced me to one of the general foremen (or some other position). I mentioned how very important Bethlehem had been to us. The foreman assured me that the men like Don were very valuable, because they were willing to work holidays and weekends, and on short notice, when the "regulars" wanted to be off.

I often referred to Bethlehem steel as "my rock." It was instrumental in making it financially possible to carry out our "10-year-plan." (What that plan was escapes me, but I don't think it included five children in eight years.) It did include staying financially afloat, buying a small home and most importantly, that Don complete his Master's degree in the required time. In addition, I thought I would describe one of the "unexpected checks" and emphasize the relationships before I put this to rest.

Don had his tonsils removed during the first year and was off from Bethlehem for a few weeks. We were so surprised when he received a disability check in the mail. We had no idea of that benefit, which helped with the loss of income.

Additionally, I did not mention the long-term

friendships formed. Jack and Liz Foster are our daughter Diane's godparents. We are Jack and Liz's son, Jay's godparents, and we also were in Jack and Liz's wedding. Not only that, but I'm sure our son, David, is eternally grateful to you, Mike, for recommending him for the teaching position at Canisius High School.

I used to say that Bethlehem Steel "gets in your blood", for Don briefly considered applying for the 'looper program', where college graduates were able to enter technical training for supervisory positions.

I think the camaraderie of the college young men in similar situations helped them keep up such a horrendous schedule. The wives supported them emotionally and "picked up the slack" at home by taking on more of the responsibility for raising the children. It did get lonely at times and interfered with family time. However, in retrospect, it appears that Bethlehem Steel was our only alternative to make possible our goals."

Jim McLaughlin, now retired Col. James McLaughlin of the US Army, was a second-generation open-hearth worker. His father, Jim, was a first helper and a melter in the open hearth while we worked there. Bethlehem for him was a family tradition and not putting in a good day or night's work would have been dishonorable to him. He had a very structured sense of what was appropriate.

Jim was a formal young man. Six foot tall, crew cut with a thin and angular physique, he exuded good health. He seemed always to stand at attention, even

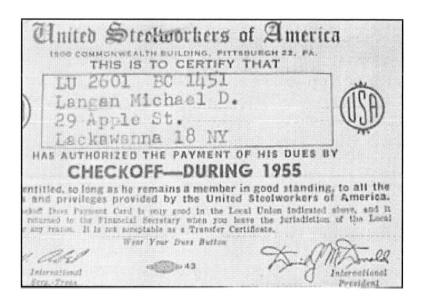

A UNITED STEEL WORKERS OF AMERICA "CHECK OFF" UNION CARD
USED BY THE AUTHOR IN HIS EIGHT YEARS AT BETHLEHEM STEEL.
THE UNION TOOK $5.00 PER MONTH OF EACH WORKER'S WAGES.

when relaxed. I wondered if he didn't sleep at attention. He had a good sense of humor but he kept it under control, even though it seeped out on overnight shifts from time to time. A few years younger, I learned discipline from Jim, and how to keep my mouth shut at work. Jim never complained, no matter how onerous the job. He just kept quiet and got things done.

'Getting things done" is what I did in the mid and late 1950s. These were years when school and work took up all of my time non-stop. Nevertheless, I noticed even then, among all the other distractions of life, that there were signs of things not going well for Bethlehem Steel.

One of the signs of the times that made my mother furious was the pink dust from the blast furnaces that settled on our clothes when they hung out on the line in our backyard on Apple Street. When there wasn't much dust on my clothes, times were bad.

Another indicator of trouble to come was the construction of the Father Baker Bridge, a concrete and steel erector set rising right in front of #1 Gate at the Lackawanna plant. The Baker Bridge steel came from another country, not from Bethlehem. It made a worker wonder what kind of a world we lived in when steel could be produced thousands of miles away and then shipped to Lackawanna more cheaply than rolling girders out the gate for the project.

It was the same story with steel billets made in #3 open hearth. According to Eddie Seifert, Ford Motor Company bypassed Bethlehem billets at the Ford Stamping Plant that made cars across the street from Bethlehem Steel's Lackawanna plant. Once again, bidding on contracts by Bethlehem Steel came a cropper - somebody else got the job.

In another instance, in the recollection of Eddie Seifert, he and Art Sambucci, both labor representatives, went to Albany to lobby the governor's office, occupied by Hugh Carey, for New York State contracts for steelmaking. According to Seifert, the two came back to Lackawanna with a multi-million dollar contract promised. Seifert said, however, that at this point, Bethlehem bigwigs re-directed the contract to another Bethlehem plant out of state instead.

In retrospect, it might be said that this kind of

haggling over 'who shot John' so many years later doesn't mean very much. This is probably true. However, insofar as the old timers' stories aggregate to form a pattern of behavior that can be confirmed by independent sources and that culminated in the dumping of the plant onto a slagheap of irrelevance, it bears more than mere mentioning.

Another 'old-timer' who knew the territory was Bill McShane, the last living superintendent of #2 open hearth, which he supervised from 1969 - 1976. McShane put 32 years in at the plant, supplanting his father, "Old Bill", who was there when I began in 1955, retired and died in 1977.

'Young' Bill McShane went to Canisius College after WW II and had kind, thoughtful memories about many of those old melters like Dave Kemp and Jimmy Hixon. He also recalled the remark of news-paper columnist Walter Winchell, who reputedly said that he'd rather have been Mayor of Lackawanna than New York City, because of the graft. I had heard this remark years ago, as well. "Young Bill" retired after working a final two years at the BOF in January 1978.

Bill mentioned that his younger brother, Bob McShane, who died at age 78, and who worked for seven years on the narrow gauge, had an article about the importance of work at Bethlehem's Lackawanna plant in his file of important documents when he died.

Boilermakers before breakfast mightn't have been on anybody's diet for good nutrition on those early Friday mornings all those years ago. From a distance, however, they did no great harm. We got our checks cashed and enabled the members of the old bull gang to push away from the bar. We had a few bucks in our pockets and that enabled us to reach for some Bethlehem-backed dreams in life - some of which were achieved and, some not.

Chapter 5: Strikes and Layoffs

Strikes and layoffs were almost as common as 'good heats', that is, steel made to specification at Bethlehem, when I worked there from 1955 - 1963. We took the layoffs in our stride, never dreaming of a complete shutdown.

The result was that I became adept at finding other work to make money while waiting for Bethlehem Steel's personnel office to call me back.

Being out of work was expected, never enjoyed, by Bethlehem workers over decades in Lackawanna. Adjacent industries, too, cut their costs this way when orders slowed and their employees added to the hoards of job seekers.

My father experienced the same uncertainty in finding a job he could keep. He became a rookie cop after WW II, one of his many jobs that included selling cars, working as a fireman, a fire inspector and even sewing seams on rugs for a department store. (While he had this last job, I rode my bike every summer's day over the bridge to the warehouse, where he worked, to bring him his lunch in a bag. I could never figure out why he didn't take it with him in the morning, but I was afraid to ask.)

#2 Open hearth is in the middle of the picture with 11 smokestacks: Furnaces 21-30.

Photo: Steelways Magazine, Bethlehem Steel.

In 1957, two years after I began working at Bethlehem, steel production fell to a three-year-low, with only 21 of 35 open-hearth furnaces running. Layoffs were moderate because the plant ran on a four day a week schedule.[31]

Like my father, I had different jobs in the intervals when I wasn't punching the clock at Bethlehem. For a few months in 1957, I rode 'shotgun' as the attendant on the Our Lady of Victory ambulance with the driver, Bruce Dickensen, a WW II Naval medic. What training I got was courtesy of Bruce and Mrs.

Minnie Rogers and Mrs. Janet Rodman, emergency room nurses and a new Portuguese doctor at the hospital, Dr. Manuel Esperanca, who became a good friend. The three of us had a number of near-death experiences; not all involving the patients, given Bruce's erratic driving.

In fact, the first time I went out on the ambulance, a young Black boxer nicknamed "Snowflakes" shot pawnshop owner Joe Kaufmann in a hold up. Joe ran his shop down the 'other end' of Lackawanna, in the 1st Ward, near the plant. Snowflake's former teacher, a woman from a Buffalo public school, accompanied him in a get-away car parked outside the pawnshop. (In time, both were arrested, tried and convicted for the crime.)

When Bruce, Dr. Esperanca and I came on the scene, Kaufmann lay dying on the floor of the store, with a bullet fired at close range into his forehead. A Lackawanna cop, already there, stood over Joe, stanching the blood spurting from his head with a roll of toilet paper. Joe's wife was screaming, hands to her face, behind the counter. Kaufmann's blood seeped up his white shirt as he lay on the floor.

I jumped over the body with the gurney. I slipped on the blood, by then a red river, sticky and making a run across the linoleum out the door. Joe's blood smeared my new Canisius baseball jacket.

"Damn", I remember thinking, then taking back the imprecation as I realized Joe's circumstances. Years later, I looked at that burgundy smear on the leather arm of the jacket, remembering this scene.

Anyway, when we got back to Our Lady of Victory Hospital, it was clear that Kaufman was dead. Inside the ER, Bruce examined the bullet wound in Joe's head, running his finger around the perimeter. "Clean job," he said.

Then, "We can't help any more here," Bruce shrugged. "Let's get some spaghetti for dinner at the Hotel Lackawanna." That was Bruce, solicitous when necessary, brutally indifferent after the fact. I couldn't eat a thing.

In its own way, riding the ambulance was as jarring as working in the open hearth. Women had babies in the ambulance, not making it to the hospital. Some people died in their houses, but we put them in the ambulance to avoid the hysterics of loved ones waiting for the medical examiner and undertaker.

One time, an open-hearth foreman's wife drank iodine in her house, trying to commit suicide because of her husband's infidelity. When we arrived, we gave her the antidote for iodine and she furiously spit it out on my baseball jacket. She didn't want to live, but she did. Spittle and blood were my middle name.

Other ambulance runs come to mind. One time, we picked up an old guy who had a heart attack in bed. He wouldn't leave the apartment until we could locate his wooden leg, which he had stowed in the closet. We had to strap the leg on before he would get on the stretcher. Even in emergencies, appearance is an important factor for victims.

Another ambulance heart attack victim who had

the last name, of all things, "Angst", meaning anxiety, flipped over onto me in the back of our speeding ambulance near Sisters' Hospital on Main Street. Angst couldn't breathe, even though I was administering oxygen to him with a mask. The flipping was his act of desperation as he suffocated.

I banged on the window of the ambulance to alert Bruce. As a result, we didn't make a long drive back to Our Lady of Victory. We took him for a quick shot of adrenaline into his chest cavity at Sisters' Hospital ER. He died anyway.

During the winter, we got an ambulance call from the other end of town, the 1st Ward again, near the plant. A woman was about to have a baby. The house was a shabby dump. At least six other people, all sleeping side-by-side and snoring on the floor, inhabited the warren where she would give birth if we didn't pick her up. I asked a big guy sleeping next to her if the groaning woman was his wife. This was a stupid question. He acted as if he didn't know her.

Another time, two prostitutes fighting over a customer got into a knife fight in a bar near the plant. When we arrived with the ambulance, a white woman in her forties sat at the bar. Her cheeks were sliced open, as were her bosoms and an area above her waist slashed by a razor. She told me her name was Joni James, also the name of a popular singer of ballads in the 1950s.

Joni wore a tight black dress over an out-sized frame cut to ribbons by the assailant. Slabs of fat on Joni's face were hanging off. Her breasts and her body fat beneath her breasts burst through the dress like the innards from an overcooked sausage.

"You got to go to the hospital, Joni", I said.

"Not until I finish my whiskey," Joni said, sitting among her razor slits, at the bar. She was tough, in no hurry, and got hundreds of sutures by the time she exited the emergency room.

When I wasn't riding the ambulance at Our Lady of Victory, I assisted in the Emergency Room. I gave a suture or two in the middle of the night on the scalp of a drunk, advised on hemorrhoids when a patient in agony thought I was a young intern and, often, delivered heavy green oxygen cylinders to patients who needed them in the hospital. I never trained for any of these jobs, other than to watch someone else do them. Interns got training, but I never did. Nobody gave me permission to do any of these things. I just did them after I knew how. I realize how stupid this is now, but it seemed second nature to me then.

These were the years before oxygen had fixtures built into the walls of the hospitals. Usually, I'd roll a cylinder of oxygen onto a dolly, take it up the elevator, hook it up to a tent in the patient's room, and set the gauge of the oxygen intake, per the doctor's orders. A nurse would always check what I was doing.

One night a young guy whom I knew by sight from the open-hearth checked into the hospital with pneumonia. I had to hook up the oxygen in his room.

I didn't know his name, but I saw him every day while working in #2 shop. He was dark, with curly hair and a heavy beard, maybe twenty-five years old.

He was a switchman on the narrow gauge railroad. This narrow gauge worked on smaller than normal railroad tracks and pushed scrap on buggies into the open hearth from the yards outside all three shops. The switchman would stop the narrow gauge engineer with a wave, pull up on the knuckle that connected the cars, disconnect some and park them in a place where the charging machine operator could get at them and begin emptying scrap into the furnaces.

I'd wave to the switchman while doing one of my jobs on the floor of the shop, as a third helper, or bull gang member. He'd wave back. That was the extent of our recognition of the other.

Therefore, it came as a shock for me to see him, wheezing, hardly drawing breath, with the overgrown beard partly covering the white sheet in bed. I fumbled about with the equipment near the head of the bed. I knew he recognized me and probably wondered what I was doing in his room. I connected the oxygen tank hoses to his tent and then began to adjust his oxygen, per instructions.

"What the f...k you doin'?" he pleaded. "You don't know nuttin' about this stuff, kid. You son of a bitch, you're killin' me," he wheezed.

What could I do? I smiled my most benign, half-professional smile, nodded and got the head nurse into the room immediately. It wasn't long before the switchman died, but I didn't feel guilty about it. Even though he thought I screwed up his oxygen, I didn't. I checked things out with the nurse to make sure I made the proper adjustments.

Another time, I was called up to another hospital floor because an elderly woman patient, confused or a bit daft, lifted a light-weight stucco statue of Jesus off its pedestal and carried it back into bed with her. I had to wrest Jesus from under her covers and put him back where he belonged.

Maybe the hardest duty I had was pretending to do something that I didn't think was my job. Unless I misunderstood the command from the nurse on duty one snowy evening - there were many no-shows for work when it snowed - a nurse directed me to bring a kit of supplies for a catheterization into an old gent's room.

Naturally, this frightened him. It frightened me. I thought I was supposed to do the catheterization, but I didn't know how and I didn't want to hurt the old guy. (I should have said this to the nurse, but didn't.)

"So," I said to the old guy, "Go into the bathroom and insert that tubing into your you-know-what." He looked at me the way a dog looks at an owner who is in the habit of hitting him with the newspaper. He could barely get out of bed. I didn't think he'd be able to handle the job.

I went back to the nurse and informed on the guy - and on myself. We couldn't do it, not even dividing the job among ourselves.

Of course, the nurse thought I was balmy. She laughed and said she didn't want me to perform the catheterization, only to bring the supplies to his room. I told the old guy this, and he was relieved, in a manner of speaking, for a little while.

Layoffs came and went. Another time, I had to keep working while laid off at the plant because of my college expenses. There were no loans from the government. Only once did I have to ask Ed Walsh, the Canisius College business manager, for an extension on my tuition. That was enough. I never did it again.

I waited in a line outside Walsh's office to plead for more time to pay my tuition. Upon entry, it was hard to see Walsh. He smoked a cigar that be-clouded his office with a heavy blue cloud.

"I'd like an extension of a couple weeks more to pay my tuition, Mr. Walsh. I think I'll be called back to Bethlehem," I coughed.

"We ain't a charity hospital here, kid," he said. His look said 'no', but he nodded, made a note in his ledger and gave me the two weeks I asked for.

In 1957, Walsh was an old geezer with grey hair and a big belly in a three-piece suit. Walsh looked like the old time actor, Charles Coburn. He was a friend - growing up in New York City in the 1920s - with Taps Gallagher, long time basketball coach at Niagara University. They were tough characters.

Some time later Taps Gallagher, basketball coach at Niagara University for years, told me about his friend, Walsh. Also, Taps had an interest in telling me the qualities of prospective athletes, because I was Director of Admissions at Niagara from 1965 - 1968.

As we walked in the Student Center at Niagara, Taps, a great storyteller, told me how he decided which basketball players got which scholarships. He said, "I walk into a classroom with a prospect and offer him a chewy caramel. If he takes the wrapper off, he gets an academic scholarship. If he eats the candy with the cellophane on, I give him an athletic scholarship."

Still another job while I was laid off at Bethlehem was courtesy of my father, who put in a word for me, at Lackawanna City Hall. It was a patronage position. I wrote about the job in The *Pittsburgh Post-Gazette*.[32] The story went this way.

****

"More than half a century ago, I was reminded that people who are elected to political jobs have to figure out how to satisfy those who support them.

My father, who fancied himself an artist, painted signs for an aspiring councilman in Lackawanna, N.Y. "Elect What's His Name" posters lay propped on the back of chairs throughout our second-floor flat for about a month. When our guy won he offered me a job as a garbage collector. It was an offer I suppose he thought I'd refuse.

I didn't.

I was willing to do just about anything to make some money while I went to college. I was disappointed, though. I thought of doing exotic research that would somehow separate the poor from their shackles, not their garbage.

But I needed a job.

My mother was against it. She had only one experience with City Hall, and it wasn't good. A dog had bitten my ten-year-old sister the previous year. My mother called the dogcatcher and reported the incident. The dogcatcher's advice was memorable for its finality.

He said, "Watch the little girl for a few days. If she gets sick, the dog has rabies." This neat assessment stole all confidence from my mother.

So she told my father to 'make another call to the councilman' and he did.

The councilman explained that the 'garbage letter' was meant to test the resolve and determination of his followers. He told my father that those who objected to it were "real fighters," strivers he wanted on his side when the going got tough.

The second patronage job I got was better. The councilman made me a stationery engineer. I wasn't going anywhere, so it sounded wonderful.

I reported to a small cinderblock-pumping house for the water authority in early December. It had snowed and I was to take the place of Mr. Kaminski on the 3-11 PM shift. The pump house was in the middle of a big field off Abbott Road.

I didn't know what to do when I showed up for work. Mr. Kaminski was leaving the building as I arrived. Mr. Kaminski smoked a pipe and looked about 90.

Soon I realize the importance of the pipe. The smell of the sanitary sewers was overwhelming. Mr. Kaminski endured it through a combination of pipe smoke and wine, which he carried in a twisted brown bag in his overcoat.

As he left, Mr. Kaminski gave me the key to the door. "What should I do?" I asked.

"Nothin", he said. "Don't do nothing."

He said I was to relieve him on the job. It was a strangely appropriate verb, I thought.

"Just sit there in the chair", he said.

The burgundy chair had the sins of generations on it, with stuffing popped out. There I sat in a foul-smelling icebox. The automatic pumps hummed. I tried to read some of Henry James's novella, "The Europeans", to the whirr of the effluents as they coursed through the pipes.

Another pump sat in the corner, not running. It was the 'safety' pump, to be started up, powered by gasoline, if the other pumps failed.

About a week into my new job, I came to work finding a huddled group of men standing and kneeling around the pumps in what looked like an elaborate religious ritual. They were whispering and trying this and that with wrenches and things.

Mr. Dombrowski, the boss, cursed. I hung at the back of the crowd with my lunch and book, feeling useless. The automatic pumps had broken down, and they couldn't get the gas pump to work. Mister D jiggered with the choke. Others changed spark plugs. They checked the oil. Nothing worked.

Mr. Dombrowski sat back a minute, thinking. He lit up a cigarette. His relaxing was a signal for the political appointees to take it easy, too.

Listlessness filled the stench-filled building. I put down my lunch on the burgundy chair, and spied a gas tank in the corner. I picked it up and brought it over to the pumps. Mr. Dombrowski brightened.

"Good work, Mike. You college boys are smart, once in a while." He checked the tank and saw that it was empty. After filling it, there were murmurs of approval from Mr. D's sycophantic helpers. I was pleased.

I took everything in silently. As the men drifted off to their next non-assignment, I took my new pipe out of my jacket and sat down to "The Europeans" with a new confidence.

I had a small bottle of white wine from Gallivan's liquor store and a baloney sandwich. It was heaven, except for the smell.

Then, just before Christmas, I received notice that my job was liquidated. No money. A life of politics was not for me."[33]

****

Retirement in the 1950s seemed the equivalent of death to me. Men I knew who retired expired like fireflies at dawn when they stopped working. How frequent it seemed that an old first helper or second helper who never missed a shift, or who came in to give an early relief for years, died within months of retirement.

When I asked about this, co-workers said the retiree began to drink more because he had nothing to do all day. Other times, some accruing sickness took its toll. Whatever the case, many seasoned, hard-working older men didn't last long in retirement.

Sickness or death among younger workers seems a newer phenomenon. In the 1950s and 1960s, layoffs usually didn't last very long. From the 1970s to the present day, layoffs have taken place and in many cases, workers never return to their jobs. It is estimated in 2010 that as many as one-third of the existing jobs from which people have been laid off disappear for good.

The result is that there are a large number of men and women subsisting on hope and federal and state handouts. The infrastructure supporting them during an increasingly long interval is not intended for long-term unemployment.

A *New York Times* article (February 25, 2010)[34]

cites the apparent correlation between job loss and death among younger workers. In a front-page story, headlined "At Closing Plant, Ordeal Included Heart Attacks", writer, Michael Luo, gives some anecdotal material of younger men, Bob Smith, 42, a forklift operator, Don Turner, 55, a crane operator, dying of heart attacks. The supposition of the article is that "the trauma of losing their jobs might have played a roll."[35]

Luo points to research that indicate layoffs affecting life expectancy, particularly a Columbia University paper by Till von Wachter and Daniel G. Sullivan, who examined death records and earning data in Pennsylvania during the early 1980s recession. This finding hardly seems surprising. Scientific studies often verify what common sense long ago concluded. This is not bad science, only tardy science.

The decade of the 1950s, the time of my high school and college careers and work at the plant and for the city of Lackawanna, were parlous times, a foretelling of still further strikes, layoffs and regrettably, the plant closing in 1982.

Chapter 6: Canisius College and Bethlehem Steel: Uneasy Partners

The decade of the 50s is memorable for another reason: One of the most remarkable people I met soon after beginning college was a student named Frank Kuhn. My sisters called him "Rac" Kuhn, because his dark, shrouded eyes made him look like a raccoon. If anything, after I got him a job at Bethlehem, his eyes got darker with silica from the mixer at the open hearth.

In 1955, I was 18 and my sister Susan was 14. This was the first time Susan met my friend, Frank. I had begun college and was working nights at Bethlehem Steel.

Frank came off a farm in southern Erie County, direct to the school. He seemed a kind, thoughtful person, not used to the machinations of the larger world. Some people might say Frank was a little short on looks. As my sister Susan would say later, he made Abe Lincoln look genteel.

I saw him for the first time at the start of my freshman semester. He walked across from Sears, back toward Canisius' Old Main building. He seemed agitated as he hulked along.

"It's not right," he said.

"Need some help?" I asked, introducing myself as we walked.

"A man saw me going into Sears and asked me what I was looking for. I told him my Dad gave me money to buy a suit when I left the farm - cause I was going to college."

The man said, "How much money you got?" I told him, "twenty dollars," Frank sighed.

"You can't get no suit for that," the man said. I got a suit in this box that's worth sixty dollars and I'll let you have it for twenty, though. The reason I'm sellin' it is that it don't fit me, but it'll fit you," he said.

"So I bought it," Frank explained. "But when I opened it and looked at it later, there wasn't any suit inside the box. Just dirty old work trousers."

This was how Frank and I met. At his best and worst, he was the most uncomplicated, trusting person I'd ever known. His honesty made you ache for him.

"Where are you living?" I asked.

"I don't have a place in the city yet," Frank said.

I asked Frank to dinner at our second floor flat in Lackawanna that night. Earlier in the evening, I took him downstairs and introduced him to our land-lady, Mrs. Williams, who lived on the first floor of our house on Apple Street. Frank took the back bed-room in her flat.

I also talked to Mike Dolan at Bethlehem, and he got Frank a job at No. 2 Open Hearth on a schedule like mine, so that Frank could go to college during the daytime.

These arrangements seemed to work out, with one exception. Mrs. Williams gave Frank her back room for $10 a week. She told him he could use the bathroom, but not the kitchen. This bothered Frank. He'd wonder about it late at night, when we'd stop at Elmer's tavern. Elmer's was a little spot on Electric Avenue, just across from Apple Street, where we lived. We'd drift into Elmer's, to have a beer on our night off.

As we sat at the bar, he tested Mrs. Williams' logic on me.

"You can use the bathroom but not the kitchen." Now what good does that do?" he asked. "If you use one, you gotta use the other, don't you, Mike? If you put something in, it's gotta come out, right?"

His banter was humorous, but I treated the complaint seriously. However, I didn't find his biologic quibbling worth defending. Mrs. Williams' prohibition seemed simple. She didn't want another person in her kitchen while she and her daughter were eating; that was all.

It was a matter of privacy and not insult. Frank knew this, too. But he was from a farm, with nine brothers and sisters, where privacy was a luxury less enjoyed. In the end, he accepted Mrs. Williams' dictum and ate in his room, on the run, sometimes even in his rusted out old '48 green Plymouth on the way to work or school.

I introduced Frank to my mother and two sisters,

Susan and Beatrice. Because the girls were younger and playful, they occasionally made fun of Frank. There jests weren't too far out of place, although they bordered on being unkind.

Frank looked like a young wrestler. His clothes ill suited him, but he was always clean and presentable. The girls could barely muffle their laughter when he'd stop upstairs to check on homework with me, or wait in the warmth of our kitchen, enjoying this forbidden area, while I got my jacket and headed out to Elmer's Tavern with him.

If Frank noticed my sisters' sly faces, he never let on. He was stoic in the face of adversity. His old car gave him opportunity to test his equanimity. A farm friend gave him the car to pay a fifty-dollar debt he owed. The car ran, but that was about all. It had a bathrobe sash holding its right door shut and the accelerator pedal was a sort of amputee's stump where the pedal should have been.

When Frank drove, he just raised and lowered his foot on the stump to go faster or slow down, as if he was keeping time to the music at a hoedown. Powering the car was a matter of delicacy with boots on, when snow and ice became encrusted underfoot. But it didn't bother Frank.

He and I picked up some college friends early one crisp morning, on the way to school. Traveling tandem helped pay for the gas, which cost 32 cents a gallon. Frank was the ultimate democrat, though; everybody could ride money or no. The car pool included me, Jocko Shea, and Saleh Assad, a counselor at Father Baker's home for orphan boys. We also picked up Michael Boyle, a senior at the college. Mike had more money than we had and rarely needed a ride. When he did cadge one, he'd squeeze into the Plymouth wearing his camel hair coat, pigskin gloves, black Eisenhower homburg and white silk muffler.

Boyle grew fond of Frank and, sensing he needed clothes, gave him the winter outfit he wore after a month of occasional rides. Boyle got a new coat, smarter than the first, with a fur collar. Frank was proud of his new possessions. He'd wear them at night to Elmer's Tavern.

In fact, Frank made an elaborate display of cleaning out the inside of a wine glass he had cadged from Elmer's bar top with his new white muffler. Then he'd pour some grape wine from the veiny cream-colored bottle he brought with him, hidden inside his coat.

Elmer would raise hell about this, because Frank never did buy anything to drink.

"You bum! You come in only to sit at the table in the front window and drink from your own bottle wearing that Republican hat," Elmer shouted at Frank as he stomped his Camel cigarette on the worn wooden floor behind the bar.

I ordered a couple of 14-ounce schupers of Phoenix Pale Ale, and Elmer's cursing subsided.

The tempo of life was predictable, if headlong: classes in the morning via the rattletrap Plymouth, then a swerve through town to Bethlehem Steel for a 3 PM - 11 PM shift with the labor gang in the open hearth, topped off by a nightcap at Elmer's after the shift was done. The routine varied with 11 PM - 7 AM shifts thrown in unpredictably, depending upon the needs of the workforce at the plant.

One winter morning the cadence varied disastrously. The Buffalo snow off Lake Erie was fierce. Men couldn't get into work at Bethlehem. We picked up Jocko, Sal and Michael Boyle. Poor Jocko had grown so fat that he had to take my seat in the front of the car.

Ice formed everywhere. As a result, we skidded to a stop on Humboldt Parkway near the college, just inches from the back flap of a heavy truck stopped ahead of us at a red light. Sal sat in the back seat, behind Frank.

For some reason, Sal and Frank always argued as we drove to school. It wasn't heavy duty bickering, more like a kind of teasing that turned to arguing, about everything.

Metaphysics was their favorite topic. It was a strange topic for Frank, but he warmed to it quickly. In the middle of a disagreement about Cartesian dualities (I don't think people dispute about this much anymore), Sal, who had a quick temper, raised his leg and, as if to punctuate a point he was making, planted a dirty, wet boot impress on Frank's back, midway between his shoulders.

The Cartesian jackboot retort made a spectacular imprint on Frank's semi-new camel hair coat. Frank looked remarkable from behind - as if someone stepped on him on his way to somewhere more important. Frank was furious.

At first, Frank maintained admirable control of the car's accelerator stump. But as Frank turned to punch Sal in the chest, the car lurched forward. The Plymouth lurched exuberantly, like a frisky dog, glad to be off the leash in the snow. We slammed into the truck sitting directly ahead of us. The truck's rigid metal flap shattered the front car window, sending a sparkling flurry of glass shards all over Jocko and Frank.

"Damn, double damn," Jocko shouted, flipping fragments of glass from his lap and books. "I even got glass in the sandwiches my aunt packed for me," he said.

Luckily, none of us was hurt. Someone countered with more fractious language. Even Michael Boyle, proper as he was, injected a surprised "My-Oh-My!"

The truck driver got out of his vehicle and surveyed the damage. The wind and snow whipped around his whiskered face. He just chuckled as he looked in at Jocko.

"A broken window is what you punks deserve," he said, pulling his hat flaps over his ears. With that gesture, he was off. We didn't even get his license plate number in the numbing cold.

We drove the rest of the way to the college in silence, glass blanketing the inside of the car and snow blowing into the vehicle, making it a miniature North Pole. The windshield wipers still worked, but they were useless, flailing wildly at snowflakes that rushed by them into the car. We made our way to class, an activity that seemed anti-climactic at best.

Frank wasn't a good student. He was very bright in some ways, particularly his acute moral sense. Part of the problem was that he needed more sleep than did I. He often got it during lectures.

It was a fact that we worked hard on the night-shifts, making 'special heats.' These special heats included ingredients that would be called for in making a particular kind of steel heat, for example, a rail steel, hardened by its properties. These ingredients were dumped via a chute into a ladle of steel that contained 200 - 250 tons of molten metal.

We would be required to make three special heats in 8 hours. This meant lifting, shoveling, grinding, loading into wheelbarrows about 12,000 pounds worth of materials.

"Quit when you're finished, boys," Jim McCann, the turn foreman would say. Fat chance we'd finish. We would lift huge chunks of manganese, low carbon chrome and phosphorus - 35 to 50 pounds each - raise them chest-high, and throw them into a grinding machine patented in 1904. Then we'd shovel up the crushed material that came out of the grinder and load wheelbarrows with 600-pound loads.

Finally, we would lift and push the barrows another 30 yards, across the front of the furnaces and around the back, to the pit side, where we'd dump the contents into a chute, awaiting loading into the ladle's molten steel, enabling the melter to assure that each 'heat' met chemical specifications for its intended use.

This heavy, six-hour finish was always our goal. Then we might sleep for an hour toward the end of the 11 PM - 7 AM shift. Somehow, Frank grew embalmed when we followed this routine.

In fact, he fell into such a deep trance one time that other workers put him on a thermal couple carrier that looked like a hospital gurney, tied him with rope, and made him look like a battering ram. They wheeled him right under the time clock, where hundreds of workers, including the superintendent, punched in for the morning shift.

Once, smart aleck workers even lit Frank's shoes with a match, to give him a hotfoot while he slept. He never woke up. Frank had a powerful way of concentrating on sleep when he put his mind to it.

Frank did have his bursts of energy, engined by his honesty. One time, during the first winter we worked in the steel plant, Frank worked a double shift, sixteen hours, because people couldn't get to work on the 11 - 7 shift, owing to a blizzard.

The foreman sent Frank to work on the dockside of the plant, unloading boxcars. The turn foreman told him that he had to start unloading 200-pound sacks of cement from a boxcar. Three men were supposed to be able to unload one car in eight hours, but the other two guys never showed up.

With his usual earnestness, Frank dug in and unloaded the whole car himself. He told me afterward he thought it was expected of him. He never stopped to eat his lunch.

The unloading became a holy crusade for him. He worked his body at frenzy pitch all night, straining and grunting as he moved the cement bags from the car. Finally, he unloaded the last sack. When it came time to go home, the foreman didn't believe that Frank had done it himself.

"Who helped you with this car, Frank?"

"Nobody, sir. I did it myself."

"Tell me who helped you or I'll make sure you get a week off for insubordination," the foreman warned him.

"I'm telling the truth. Nobody helped me. I did it myself."

So it went. The superintendent gave Frank a week off for refusing to say who helped him unload the boxcar. Frank accepted the penalty without complaining, except to say it wasn't right, and he wouldn't forget it.

Weeks turned into months, passing quickly. Shift work at Bethlehem made life a seamless garment. We'd work Friday night, 3 p..m. - 11 p.m., and then double back again the next morning, Saturday, 7 a.m. - 3 p.m.. We would work the next day shift on Sunday, first stopping off at St. Barbara's Church for Mass at 6 a.m., before work.

St. Barbara's, a Polish parish at Ridge Road near Center Street, fascinated me. It had such solemnity and dignity - even that early in the morning. The ushers wore tuxedos as they took up the collection. I felt vaguely abashed as I knelt in old work clothes, digging out a dollar in the dark that hadn't come clean from the work of the day before.

Monday night we'd work 11 p.m. - 7 a.m. and then go to school, with sleep more on our minds than classes. It was a hard struggle to get through the day awake and then drive home and nap for a while. I was very tired. Usually Frank fell asleep in the car, sometimes even as he drove. By Tuesday night, we'd shake off our lethargy around 11 p.m.. We'd stop back to Elmer's for a drink, if Frank were up to it.

Elmer's Tavern was always the same. We would have a 10-cent beer, read the *Courier Express*, the next morning's paper, talk a bit, eat a hot dog that Elmer would electrocute in his new food unit, chomp on some red-roasted peanuts and then head home. School the next morning, Wednesday, would be followed by the 3 PM - 11 PM shift and then we'd have a layover until Thursday night, when shift work would begin again.

The end of the Thursday night shift at Bethlehem was the best time of the week. It was payday! The routine of work and school was enjoyable in its own way. However, it was left to my mother to attach a moral to it.

"You boys will be glad you worked your way through school. It'll mean a lot more to you than if someone gave you the money. When you are both successful, you'll remember the effort and be glad."

I don't think that Frank or I ever thought of the experience this way. We liked Bethlehem more, not less, than college. It wasn't that college was boring or unimportant; not a bit. We knew that, long term, getting a degree was valuable. However, school wasn't as much fun as working in the steel plant. Frank and I would both have preferred a beer and a newspaper at night after work, if a choice between school and work were demanded.

The proof of the pudding was that whenever anyone at the bar asked us what we did, we always said, "Open hearth." It would have been an embarrassment to say "college student." That meant you were not grown up, not finished with adolescence.

Studying was not an activity to be endured when pot-bellied, hard-drinking men leaned forward on their stools to ask you your business. Work and study was a double life that continued throughout college and even afterward.

Of course, there were times I was so tired I couldn't think straight about things. Once I remember starting to feel sorry for myself, working and going to school. I had read the Irish writer Frank O'Connor's biography and a line from it stood out to me: "...only in the imagination do the great tragedies take place", or something like that.

From reading Irish stories, it was a short mental step to imagining things that never happened. I once conjured up in my mind's eye the tragedy of my mother's sorrow after my sudden death from overwork. It was a joke, of course, but I realized the fantasy meant I was taking myself too seriously.

In my dream, Father Phil Dobson, S.J., the dapper little Canisius President, would be at my wake, offering the dubious consolation of philosophy and a dollop of wisdom to my relatives for my premature passing.

"He was a wonderful boy," Father Dobson would say, his baldhead glistening. "The poor lad's brain seizure was brought on because of his inhuman schedule and his intense devotion to study. I should have seen it coming," Father Dobson would whisper consolingly to my mother, crippled as she was with her grief. Mother seemed to have acquired arthritis overnight.

Then in this same fantasy the #2 Open Hearth Superintendent, craggy old Bill McShane, appeared. He would tell my mother, "The poor lad was doing a calculus problem for homework while pouring steel when he was overcome." (What a crock! Anybody who ever worked on the pit-side of the open hearth would know this was impossible. McShane was pulling a Huck Finn, lying through his hat as a kindness to my grieving mother.)

Never mind. Just about this time, everyone at my wake would be overcome with grief. This was the cue for the undertaker, Tommy Mescall, to pass out the holy cards.

On each card would be a picture of our Lord praying at Gethsemane, and on the reverse side of the card would be noted my birth and death dates, along with a short exhortation written especially for me. It would be something maudlin and excessively Irish, like "It is an awful moment when gaiety dies in those who have no other hold on life."

All of this would be make-believe, of course. Great tragedies like these really do take place only in the imagination.

I have a hazy remembrance of college graduation. I bought myself a suit for the first time, with real money and not credit. We lined up to be measured for academic gowns in Father Edward Gillen's Student Personnel Office, Room 109 of the Old Main Building. The thought of donning a gown was more a relief that school was over than any real pleasure about the ceremony.

I should say a word about the 'work and study' double life that the promise of Bethlehem paychecks made possible. After college the same work routine continued 'double time', both at the plant and with my beginning a life teaching English at Lafayette High School on Buffalo's west side.

Frank and my sister Susan began courting. They married and tragically, Susan died on her honeymoon down south. Her illness was described as an attack of asthma that collapsed her lungs. Frank rushed Susan to the hospital but she did not survive. Everyone in both families was crushed by the terrible event.

Frank, who had a good soul and wanted to help people, pursued a career in social services, I think. In later years, I tried to contact him from time to time but was never successful.

Chapter 7: Bethlehem Deserts its Workers

Twenty-five years ago, Pulitzer Prize winning reporter John Strohmeyer wrote, "Lackawanna is a city without a pulse. It was severely stricken in October 1983, when Bethlehem Steel 'pulled the plug' on steelmaking in this one-industry town. An estimated 7,300 well-paying jobs in this city of 21,700 people went down the drain and the ripple effect took many others with them in one of the largest single industrial shutdowns in the nation."[36]

A 'glint' of Bethlehem's past is all that is left now. The story I wrote about the open hearth for the *Pittsburgh Post-Gazette* accentuates competition, and, in that sense, it represented the reality fifty years ago. At that time, a 'me-first' attitude ruled both inside and outside the Bethlehem Lackawanna plant. Melters in the open hearths fought each other for bonuses based on production inside the mill, while representatives of Bethlehem worked long and hard to get tax breaks from the City of Lackawanna and succeeded - to a degree.

Jim Fennie, Norm's brother, was Lackawanna's long-time senior auditor who retired in 1979. He excoriated Lackawanna's City Council at the time for, as he put it, not fulfilling its part of the bargain to give tax breaks to Bethlehem Steel. This gave the company an excuse to leave town. Jim repeated this story to me in his early nineties, before he died. However, in retrospect it isn't likely to think that Bethlehem would have stayed in any case. Whatever tax breaks the company got would not have been enough, given the rise of foreign competition.

By 1990, *The Washington Post* took note of the demise of Bethlehem in Lackawanna. In an article entitled "What Big Steel Giveth, Big Steel Can Take Away" (January 28, 1990), reporter Cindy Skrzycki wrote about Lackawanna, New York. "This is the city that big steel built and that big steel brought down."

She continued: "Since the last ingot was turned out at Bethlehem Steel Corp.'s plant here south of Buffalo almost seven years ago, the city has had an eerie stillness about it. Bars where sweaty steelworkers cashed their checks and downed "boilermakers" are gone. The legendary Father Baker Bridge, a 100-foot-high span that linked Buffalo and its northern suburbs with the plant, has been dismantled...."

Ms. Skrzycki, earlier a student at Canisius College in Buffalo when I was a vice president there, rang me up and asked if I had any reflections about Bethlehem. She quoted me, "It was a vital, active place, said Michael D. Langan, who worked in the Lackawanna plant for eight years while he was going to college and later when he started a teaching career in Buffalo. But it doesn't exist anymore."

I suppose I would amend what I told her now.

Bethlehem Steel does still exist, in my head. I think of it every day. It remains in memory - good thoughts and bad - of all those who worked there over the years and for whom it held promise.

I spent a couple of years in the early 1960s 'on salary', lighting re-built open-hearth furnaces and catching turns as a stripper foreman, usually following an experienced man, Eddie Gaughan, and responsible for stripped moulds from poured steel ingots by huge cranes. I worked with 'Loopers', a term used for those who had gone through extensive technical training to become senior supervisors with Bethlehem. They included excellent workers, Bob Allen and Don Overdorf, among others.

I had no such training. Behind me, in terms of success, were a number of years working in the open hearth and knowing people who could help me as I dealt with the normal 12-16 hour light up of a newly re-built furnace.

Lighting a furnace was not like doing a steak on an outside grill. It required knowledge of the furnace, as much as a first helper was required to know and detailed in the *First Helper's Manual*, put out by Bethlehem. It also called upon one's observation of things that might go wrong in a matter of seconds, and the capacity to call a melter, turn foreman, pipe fitter, bricklayers, or others who could remedy a problem before a catastrophe struck and resulted in an exploding furnace.

(I never had a furnace explode. It did happen to a looper, to whom I turned over the furnace. He was

AUTHOR'S COPY OF FURNACE MANUAL USED WHEN
LIGHTING FURNACES AFTER REBUILD.

busier drinking his tea than watching the furnace.
After I had gone down the stairs to the locker room to
take a shower, I heard a huge explosion. #28 furnace
had gassed up, lacking oxygen, blowing its heavy
metal doors flat out to a 180-degree angle and

spreading a rolling flame, across the floor to the furnace control board itself. The looper, standing nonchalantly in front of the furnace, got his face burned, and he dropped his tea. He also got two weeks off, 'on the beach' as they used to say, without pay.)

I handled lighting furnaces, but it was tough. I wished that I had more technical experience. I developed canker sores in my mouth from worrying about getting things right. Of great help was Nils Gunnersen, an experienced furnace man who was very knowledgeable.

I thought about all this after Skrzycki wrote her piece on the demise of Bethlehem Steel in Lackawanna. I offered my own reflection in *The Buffalo News* on February 5, 1990, remembering those years in the 50s and 60s when I worked at the plant.

****

In it I reflected, "Somehow, the mind keeps alive past experiences with searing acuity. No matter how long ago events might have occurred, if they meant something, they can be recalled...I picture in my mind's eye hundreds of steelworkers: names, faces and expressions.

I see again the way each man tames that huge, cavernous environment. One does it with a verbal order, another a clever maneuver with a bulldozer, a third with the swing of a shovel, still another with the deft touch on instruments of the charging machine or overhead crane. There in front of the furnace, the melter recalculates figures to make the specifications of a heat of steel come out "right on the button."

I remember slouching toward Bethlehem from the parking lot in the early dawn, approaching that dark, faceless place where showers of steel dart weightless to surprise us, then settle gurgling into ladles, holding 250 or 300 tons of molten steel. Tapping a furnace is so hot and dangerous that the second helper's woolen coat, cap and gloves sometimes catch fire. It gets my attention.

In my imagination, Bethlehem Steel is always new. It challenges, I see it for the first time, each time. As a young college student, I thought men from the open hearth were larger than life. They seemed great men, well known, respected and relied upon at the plant because of their mental and physical strengths....

The names of those I summon up in my recollection from the open hearth - and I suspect it's the same for other departments of the plant - sound like a secular litany. Norm Fennie, "Big Bill" McShane, Chuck Thebo, Eddie Lorenzi, George Brenner, Carl Norbeck were superintendents of open hearths. Mike Dolan, Dave Kemp, Jim and Bob McCann, Bob Mulholland, John Luther, Paul Lafey, Eddie Gaughan, Joe Beiber, Mickey Parczewski and Mike Flak were melters and foremen.... As I reflect on it, I was very lucky. To be in such a place was like having a hundred foster-fathers. They poured out their lives, like the molten metal they made, for family friends and an industry they loved. Best of all, the country prospered.

POURING A HEAT OF STEEL FROM A LADLE INTO MOULDS.
PHOTO: STEELWAYS MAGAZINE, BETHLEHEM STEEL.

Now the steel industry has deserted them," I concluded. "Only their memory and what they did remain, still vital and alive, with the passing of time. There is no beating it back."

****

How time changes things! In 1900, life was different on the eastern shore of Lake Erie. Buffalo was a leading port, a gateway to the west, full of promise. It was a flour manufacturer and a railroad hub. The Buffalo area that included Lackawanna developed into a major city because of hydroelectric power and the growth of heavy industry, represented by Bethlehem Steel, Hanna Furnace and the automakers, Ford and Chevy.

At that time, Buffalo was a melting pot with more than sixty nationalities living side by side. Occasionally newcomers fought with others as they jostled for social and economic position and Irish cops interceded. Verlyn Klinkenborg wrote a book about Buffalo and one of its inhabitants, his father-in-law, Eddie Wenzek. Called "The Last Fine Time", it touches upon this phenomenon.

In it, Klinkenborg, later a trustee of the New York Times, earlier wrote "...the saturnine do not plan cities...the little village on the Erie grew so fast that the trope of its humanity was drawn out to a nearly ludicrous extent."[37] Everything stretched, grew and then contracted in a mysterious calculus. Bethlehem Steel changed, too, in one hundred years. It went from major industry to non-entity.

Buffalo's decline was noticeable by the late 1950s. The completion of the New York State Thruway, the building of suburban developments and shopping malls moved middle class populations from the city proper into new communities like Orchard Park, Amherst and Cheektowaga. Heavy industry left the northern rust belt, including Buffalo, and repaired to the more clement - and non-unionized - southern states. Later, companies moved out of the United States entirely, because of cheaper foreign labor costs.

Western New York's leadership tried to develop new businesses instead of compensating for heavy companies that died or departed. It failed for a number of reasons. Tax issues, job decline, bad weather, rust-belt antipathies, infrastructure problems: causes were legion.

Banks, colleges, universities, medical technology and light industry could not fill the gaps alone. Younger and middle age people moved to cities where better jobs beckoned. People made the change reluctantly, hating to leave family, but with the conviction that they were doing the right thing.

In 1950, the population of Buffalo was 580,000 and it was the 15th largest city in the country. In 2008, its population was estimated to be 270,000. In 2008, Lackawanna could scrape together just over 19,000 people, less than the 20,000 that the Bethlehem plant employed there earlier, during its peak years.

These are not auspicious times for the unemployed and elderly in the Buffalo area. At the dawn of the 21st century, older people in Buffalo gaze out their windows and see run-down buildings and a decaying social infrastructure. Some await their meals-on-wheels. What makes things worse is that the taxpayers are paying higher taxes with fewer benefits to show for their money.

Times are not great for the middle aged and young of the Buffalo area, either. If you want to think about how the present came to be, you have to examine the past and Bethlehem Steel's role in it.

Trouble came to the corporation in the name of Edmund F. Martin, who was elected Chairman in 1962. Earlier, Martin ran the Lackawanna plant, ensconced in the white opulence of his office that I earlier noted. Perhaps his misplaced sense of appropriateness is best expressed by the construction in 1972 of Martin Tower, a 21-story, $35 million dollar headquarters in Bethlehem, PA. What was Chairman Martin thinking? This building was no bargain for anyone. Later, when the company was in hock, it sold the accoutrements of Martin Tower for pennies on the dollar.

Nine years later, when it was obvious that Bethlehem was in fiscal trouble, reporter John Strohmeyer quotes Martin's successor, its then Chairman, Donald H. Trautlein, as 'pulling the plug on steelmaking in Lackawanna' in 1981.

That was the same year that Trautlein received $555,986 as a bonus from the company. I suspect that it was hard for Trautlein to feel the little peoples' pain as he lopped thousands from Bethlehem's payroll. It's tough to be solicitous when you are pocketing over half a million dollars in a bonus for cutting costs.

1981 was the same year that the "…more fortunate victims in staff reductions were those persuaded to leave through financial incentives. Management level employees with an adequate combination of age and years of service were paid lump sums to take early retirement, according to John Strohmeyer in "City Without a Pulse."

The so-called 'carrots' were based on pensions that the company would have had to pay according to actuarial life expectancy. It was common to hear of supervisors leaving with a $250,000 to $300,000 lump sum. Higher echelon officers left with much more. In 1982 alone, 13 vice presidents who took "the lump" left with severance packages exceeding at least $1 million apiece.[38]

Such payouts were a million miles away from the stories I heard sitting at a wedding a few years ago and listening to an older priest at the same table who had been in high school work for years before retiring. He talked about the sense of loss that kids had getting out of high school when there was no longer any steel plant available to get a job.

Generations of families worked at Bethlehem and now, as Strohmeyer noted earlier, a priest of his acquaintance said the same thing, "The loss of the Bethlehem Steel plant has taken away hope."[39]

Well, people cope, or at least they try to do their best. When the plant closed, Lackawanna lost about

$4.1 million a year in real estate taxes, according to then Mayor Thomas E. Radich.

Not only that, but the steelworkers' union membership fell off a cliff after Bethlehem left in the early 1980s. Arthur Sambucci, the union president of Local 2603, related at the time "…only about 1,100 of the 7,300 discharged workers qualified for pensions, which ranged from about $900 to $1200 a month, depending on length of service."[40]

People like those in the past who could build a life, establish seniority for retirement and pension, buy a house or a car, afford private school tuition for their kids, join the Bethlehem Supervisors' Club, are scant in numbers today.

Here are a few examples of how hard the plants' closings, Bethlehem and Republic, hit people. The recollections are from interviews seen on the WNED TV special, *Buffalo's Voices of Steel* program.

Len Jaworski, who worked at Bethlehem's Lackawanna plant from 1967 - 1981, remembered,

"When you're making a good buck and you've got benefits and someone's offering you minimum wage with no benefits, uh, even if you went to school, uh, it, it's hard. I used the word *ugly* before, and it was *ugly*. It was, there was, it was depression, you could slice with a knife. You could see it in people. You could see it in their faces, the, uh, the righteousness and nobility of having a job was gone. And, a man or a woman that's in that situation after 15, 20, 30 years of life, uh, doesn't, all of a sudden reorient and become a computer programmer or a, a VCR repairman. Not the same.

I thought it would be easy to find a job and make that kind of money, uh, and the face of the, the nation changed. The information age came. Uh, everything changed, and, uh, the bottom fell out in the economy …, not just for me, but for a lot of people. I knew, back in the '70s …during the oil embargo, I knew people with Ph.D.s that were pumping gas. So, that reality was, uh, hey, you know, you got to eat, you got to have a place to live, what do I do now, and I'll just go over here and apply. It, it didn't happen that way for me. It was tough.

Some people drank themselves to death. Some people were walking and moving, but they were dead. Uh, a, a person without a future and a past that doesn't matter is a shell, and, uh, you could blame it on the economy, you could blame it on a lot of things, but, uh, it was *ugly*. That, that's all I can say is, it was, from a personal point of view, it was very *ugly*."

Jaworksi's remarks are valuable because they punctuate how workers who had given their all to the company felt powerless to do anything about the circumstances of a change in technology, and their being dropped from Bethlehem's employment rolls. What do you do when you can't do anything? Jaworski calls it *ugly*, and it is the perfect word for those who were 'chewed up' in the process.

Another Bethlehem worker, Tim O'Shei, heard the bad news when he was away from the plant.

"When they shut steelmaking in 1982, I was out on vacation. I heard it on television. It was, uh, that quick, the announcement of it, not the actual doing of it. The announcement came, like it always does, around Christmastime, uh, the week before Christmas, I believe it was, 1982.

I got called into work and we had to have meetings because there's procedures you have to go through when you're going to shut a place down in steelmaking. Ninety-day notification, then a 60, then a 30, and 10. There's, contractually, everything you had to do. And I had clerks all over the plant. There might be four clerks in this office; 200 in accounting and data processing; but every little area had a clerk, or clerks. I was involved in the shutdown business. And it was disheartening, uh, in '82. I, I should back up, in '77, is when they shut down Structural and I had the job as Chairman of the Grievance Committee. And one of my jobs was to sign my father's separation papers. Not easy to do."

Think about O'Shei signing his father's separation papers. If that doesn't cut 'close to the bone', what does?

All steel making facilities in the area were hit hard. Rick Coughlin worked at Republic Steel from 1978 - 1982. He said, "We ...earned pretty good. I was actually making...when I left, I bet I was making $27 an hour, I think, in 1982. The next job I took was for $5.50 an hour, and I worked at it for two years.

The job I took, though, was programming a computer. It was an Apple computer for a company

… that gave me an opportunity to write programs for them, which I had learned at the steel plant, and after a few years of doing that, eventually I ended up in a career in computers and eventually owning my own computer consulting company over the years. So, taking that step back, being willing to do what it takes to re-train yourself into something that you think has some future eventually allowed me to go, to move forward.

I had a college degree and I had a teaching degree. So, that was also a difficult time for teachers, and that was one of the reasons I didn't become a teacher when I came out of college. I went to the steel plant. I was supposed to be a teacher."

Rick Coughlin had some 'transfer of training' that he could rely upon, given his college background and capacity to move in another direction with computer work. Over the years, this became a common phenomenon for workers whom Bethlehem dropped. However, the strategy didn't work very well as more people were laid off and the economy had fewer jobs to offer.

Tom Cox, a metallurgist who worked at Bethlehem, remembered 1982.

"Oh, God, it was, it was devastating. It was really devastating. It was devastating for all of Western New York, but mostly Lackawanna, because Lackawanna, as Bethlehem Steel went, so went Lackawanna. I mean, it's hard for people to understand that Bethlehem and Lackawanna were one and the same. So, when Bethlehem Steel left,

Lackawanna became a ghost town, because people think, oh, it was just 22,000 jobs lost. Not 22,000 jobs. There were other thousands and thousands, every restaurant, tavern, mom-and-pop store, especially in lower Lackawanna, was gone.

There was no business for them because the steel plant did furnish them their living. That's where they made their living. When those guys walked out that gate, that's where they went … to the taverns, to the stores, to the restaurants. Now they're not walking out. There's nobody there. So they didn't have any, slowly but surely. If you go down over the bridge today and you walk that, and on the right side it's nothing but wasteland. It's nothing but, there's a couple of buildings here and there, but they're nothing. They're closed.

Well, one day my boss, the chief metallurgist, called me in. I didn't know what he wanted. He told me, "close the door." You want a cup of coffee. He has two assistants there. I thought I did something wrong. And I says, uh, what's up? He says, well, Tom, you know we're going to, we're closing down. I says, yeah, I've heard that and I believe it. A lot of guys didn't believe it. I believed it. And he says, and we're going to open up Johnstown. Yeah, I says, I've heard that, too. And he says, well, we need somebody to go down to Johnstown and set up the metallurgical problem, or program because they don't have one, and we talked it all over and we'd like you to be the guy to go down.

Well, I was flabbergasted. I, I was really,…, at

that point in my career, close to when I was going to be thinking about retirement. And I never thought in a million years that at my age and, and this, this situation, that they would offer me this. And like a little kid, I just took the bait, you know. I, I said, no kidding? They says, yeah, we think you're the guy to do it. So I says, well, yeah, I says, I'd, I'd, I think I can handle that, you know, blah, blah, blah.

So … they wanted me to move. They wanted me to sell the house. I said, no, I'm not going to sell my house and move to a little town down in Pennsylvania. They said, "why?" I said, well, what if you close that plant down in a year or two, what am I going to do? I'm down with a mortgage down in Pennsylvania? I said, "This house is paid for." So I said no. They said, what do you want to do? I said I'll commute. They said, Tom, it's 220-some miles. I said, I don't care, I'll commute. I'll work five days a week for you. I'll come home weekends, holidays and so forth, vacations. And I'll set up the program and in, in a year or so, I'll retire.

And they said, well, if that's what you want to do, and they treated me fine. They put me on an expense account. They had a room at the, uh, Sheraton hotel in, in, uh, Johnstown, right next to the steel plant, paid for all my meals, my transportation back and forth, everything, took care of me completely. So they treated me like a million dollars, but, but, uh, that's what I did."

Here was a good example of Bethlehem needing a job done, and Tom Cox willing to 'drive the extra miles' to handle it. Result: he was rewarded by the company.

These examples show that, depending upon time and circumstance, Bethlehem and other plants could be sensible places to make a living. For individuals, it could be a fond memory or, more often, a nightmare.

In this regard, Ed Seifert, the #2 open-hearth union boss, tells the story of how both supervisory and hourly workers lost their health insurance as the company fell into debt, got their insurance back briefly, and then had to forfeit it when the company declared Chapter 11. Fortunately, after the bankruptcy, workers were able to retain a group health category and pay the monthly charge but at a higher rate themselves that the company earlier paid at a lower rate.

Retirement was an issue, too. There were a couple different retirement plans that Bethlehem supported. One was an 'age 65 and 20 years rights' option, and an earlier choice for workers hired earlier, that offered '30 years of work and retirement' at whatever age you were when you had 30 years of employment with the company.

In 2001, with net worth of negative $15.8 million, Bethlehem Steel filed for Chapter 11 bankruptcy protection on October 17. In 2002, the U. S. Pension Benefit Guaranty Corporation took over International Steel Group of Cleveland's assets and liabilities, which included Bethlehem Steel's pensions, on December 18. Now, the government, you and me, are paying Bethlehem's pensions.

Besides Rick Coughlin and Tom Cox's descriptions of making the best of a bad situation, there was another success story that came out of the turmoil that I know about. Undoubtedly, there were more good stories than those recorded here.

Don Williams had more than 34 years at Bethlehem Steel. He managed his future because of careful preparation, hard work and perhaps some luck.

He wrote to me in early 2010, recounting his career with Bethlehem Steel and I quote some of his e-mail here.

"In the early 1950's, I recall driving on Route 5 through Lackawanna with my folks. At times, the air was reddish with smoke from the plant. I also recall being able to see into #1OH through spaces between outside wall panels and see the bright glow from the furnaces. My dad and uncle worked at the plant at that time, although not in steelmaking.

Sometime in the late 50s, our Boy Scout troop got a plant tour. (Several dads worked there). From that tour, the only memory I still have was standing on the charging floor of 2OH, probably near #30 furnace, if it was still there, and watching a heat tap into a ladle, probably #29 furnace - totally awesome. I wondered at the time what would happen if someone tossed a glass marble or coin into that cauldron! Teenage thoughts, for sure.

In 1966, I graduated from the U. of Delaware, and came back to WNY to work for Chevy at the Tonawanda Engine Plant as a management trainee. While there, they got me into the Army Reserve, for which I am properly grateful. I left Chevy 11/67 after I applied at BSCO.

The shocker came in late 1982 or early 1983, when the shutdown of the Lackawanna 'hot end', including the blast furnaces, steelmaking, and 45 x 90 slab mill was announced. The steel industry at that time had more capacity than supported by sales, and foreign steel, especially sheet steel for the auto industry, was hitting the US ports in increasing quantities.

The Lackawanna plant was able to transfer many experienced salaried employees to other surviving plants, including Sparrows Point, MD, Burns Harbor, IN, the three Pennsylvania plants at Steelton, Johnstown and Bethlehem, as well as the home office in Bethlehem.

I was fortunate to be offered a job in early 1984 at the Home office in the Purchasing Department where, because of my plant experience, I was assigned to the Reclamation Division, headed by Larry Bostic. There I sold surplus scrap iron and steel and non-ferrous metals from all the remaining plants to the trade, mostly through brokers such as Luria Bros., Ehrman-Howell and Tube City. In a touch of irony I also sold most of the scrap from the facilities tear-down now underway at Lackawanna, headed up by Eion Gordon's reclamation dept.

I remained at the home office exactly 5 years, earning a Certified Purchasing Manager certification, before being transferred back to Lackawanna as District Purchasing Agent following the retirement of Ed Casey.

I finished my career at Lackawanna, retiring in early 2002 after 34.25 years. At that time, the Coke Ovens and Galvanized Product divisions were the only remaining operations. The 13" Bar Mill was sold to Republic Steel and continued in operation, as it is today."

By now, the reader should get the point. When all is said and done, Bethlehem deserted its workers. Some got pensions while others did not. Regulations ruled. If former Bethlehem workers had transferable skills, they moved. Some of the job finding might have been a matter of luck or good connections, but most of the outplacement and job loss was the result of brutal economics. Bethlehem could not compete and left town.

The Corporation tried to hold on at its other plants, appealing to the government and to the steel-worker's union for breaks. In the end, it was not a successful strategy. The Lackawanna experience spread, and Bethlehem's president, Donald H. Trautlein, cut his own pay and everybody else's, along with shutting down marginal operations. This meant "selling off West Coast plants, spinning off all the ship repair yards", all after closing the Lackawanna plant, once the nation's fourth largest steel mill.[40]

In fact, the reduction of the Corporation's assets played out over years. In 1983, the United Steel Workers agreed to a contract that granted a 9 percent cut in wages and benefits over three years. In 1984, Bethlehem pushed for a curb in steel imports, which reached a record 26 million tons. President Ronald

Reagan set a five-year voluntary steel trade quota. It did not mean much.

In 1985, three years after the Lackawanna plant closed, Bethlehem employment stood at 51,360. LTV Corp absorbed Republic Steel and Jones and Laughlin Steel to form LTV steel, knocking Bethlehem from its #2 position as steelmaker.

In 1986, Walter F. Williams was elected chairman, promising to make the company more competitive.

In 1988, Bethlehem reported a record net income of $403 million, and modernized its Sparrows Point hot-strip mill the following year.

By 1990, Bethlehem total employment was 29,574. In 1995, the company ended steelmaking at its Bethlehem, PA plant, for the first time since 1873, turning its property into an industrial museum with the Smithsonian Institution in 1997.

About this transformation, friends of my wife and I, Nancy and Dick Traubitz, wrote to us in June of 2010, after a visit to Bethlehem, PA. Nancy observed,

"We went to Bethlehem for my 50th college reunion in late May. It's so weird. Where there were blast furnaces, now a gambling casino and lots of new buildings for Lehigh University. We walked around the old part of the Lehigh campus, where both Dick and Tom (her son), graduated. The whole city is now a tourist destination, not the vital industrial city we remembered. Little Moravian College in the historical section of town is still much as I remembered it — a few new buildings but mostly the same old buildings and the same staid German pietistic feel."

Is there anything sadder than towns opening up 'theme parks' to a forgotten age, or worse still, permitting gambling casinos that encourage baser instincts in people? The argument for gambling is that it gives whatever city in which it operates derivative income from the casino. This is a hard pill to swallow.

Back to Bethlehem's inevitable decline: In 2000, the Company reported losses of $118.4 million and was dropped from Standard & Poor's 500 index. The next year, Bethlehem Steel filed for Chapter 11 bankruptcy on October 17, with company wide employment at 13,100.

The federal government took over Bethlehem's pension obligations in 2002 and in 2003, International Steel Group purchased Bethlehem Steel's assets for $1.5 billion, putting what remained of the company out of its misery.[42]

Afterword: Buffalo's Voices of Steel

I should explain how I came to write "Tapped Out" and its relationship to *Buffalo's Voices of Steel*. In fact, these two enterprises are not related but they appear together because they were completed at the same time in fall 2010.

My wife, Joanne, for years was a steely voice suggesting that I write about my Bethlehem experience. I began "Tapped Out" a few years ago, but put it on the back burner until Andy Grant, son of long time WNED TV producer, John Grant, called me about the prospective TV program in early 2010.

My interest in "Tapped Out" has been to "keep the flame of memory lit" - in a sense, an action similar to my lighting of the re-built open-hearth furnaces. I want to memorialize the work and lives of those who toiled in the industry that I knew.

Part of this recollection enlivened when I visited the Burchfield Penney Art Center in 2009. I had a "eureka moment" as I stood in front of Buffalo artist Robert Noel Blair's watercolor (reprinted on the back cover) with pencil sketch of a place where I had spent part of eight years of my life.

The title of the work was "Bethlehem Steel, Open Hearth, Lackawanna, circa 1946-47." I wrote about it in another piece in *The Buffalo News* on November 9, 2009. Part of what I wrote follows and it parallels some of my earlier recollections of the open hearth.

****

"Blair (1912-2003), who died in the Town of Holland, south of Buffalo, was a prolific painter of rural life and World War II scenes. His work, according to "Ask/Art, the Artist's Bluebook," was noted for its color, fluidity and movement.

As I examined Blair's watercolor, my imagination took me back to 1955, to No. 2 open hearth, at the Bethlehem Steel Lackawanna Plant.

Huge metal doors lined with kiln brick were raised from a panel on the front of each furnace by the first helper, so that the charging machines and overhead cranes could drop into the bath of the furnace 200 tons of materials that would soon melt and be transformed into various grades of steel.

This detail is background to Blair's watercolor. His rendering shows the pit side of an open hearth, that is, the backside of the open-hearth floor, about 60 feet below the front of the furnaces, eight years before my working there.

In truth, if you started working in the open hearth in 1905 or 1955, there wouldn't be much difference. Nothing changed materially during those years. I remember doing "special heats" with Jim McLaughlin, three-to eight-hour shifts, each requiring 3,500 pounds of material to be lifted, ground, shoveled, wheeled and dumped in boxes behind the furnaces.

For example, two workers would grind up huge 75-pound pieces of low-carbon chrome into shards that a worker shoveled onto a pneumatic-tire wheelbarrow that weighed more than 1,000 pounds when loaded. The patent on the machine used to do the grinding in 1955 was dated 1900. (In the late 1950s, the introduction of oxygen furnaces changed the basic open-hearth operation, cutting "heat times" from eight to nine hours to three to four hours.)

I suppose if someone viewed Blair's watercolor without ever having worked in the open hearth, what would be pleasing about it would be its balance and visual acuity, the swirl of colors, orange, yellow and darker hues. The rest would be mysterious.

However, for those who have worked in the open hearth, sweat, smoke, sulfur fumes and graphite dust permeate the scene. In those days, one took work clothes home once a week in a big paper bag. That meant shirts, trousers and heavy underwear (worn to avoid slag burns), encrusted with white "Burmaroad" zigzags of salt, for wife or mother to throw into the washing machine.

Heavy work shoes, gloves, a Bethlehem Steel dark blue wool jacket, helmet or cap and dark glasses for peering into furnaces were left in what were called "overhead lockers." Think of a chain fall with a metal basket and hooks, which raised your clothes 20 feet in the air in a locker room with four showers, used 24 hours a day by 800 men.

Now to the watercolor: What is it that attracts the eye?

This will differ with the beholder. For me, the pit side crane is carrying a ladle of 200 tons of molten steel, to be poured from the left side of the painting, the platform used by the pourers, to measure out the heat into 26-by-28-inch, 28-by- 35-inch or many other variations depending upon use, open-faced molds that were 15 feet tall. They might hold two or three tons of popsicle orange bright steel after it hardened and removed by cranes overseen by the stripper foreman (another of my jobs), 10 football fields away from the pouring.

In the painting, other heats are being tapped, slag pots are fuming, railroad tracks are glistening and a lone worker is inching toward the lower level of the watercolor, perhaps to tell Al, the ladle liner, that he needs a newly lined ladle for #24 furnace before 4 a.m.

The painting shows the stark beauty of the tableau, but also the danger. It was not child's play. I stayed alive, but others didn't.

Men like brothers Jim and Bob McCann, a melter and pit foreman respectively in those years, or melters like Dave Kemp or Cy Koons, could tame that cavernous disorder with a verbal order, or a deft touch on instruments in front of a furnace, recalculating figures to make the specifications of a heat of steel come out "right on the button."

Blair has done a meticulous job of interpreting what it meant to be the middle of things on the pit side of an open hearth. If only one could purchase a copy of the painting! At present, it is not available. Alumni of Bethlehem Steel, take note. When Blair's watercolor can be purchased, it will be an immediate best seller at the Burchfield Penney Art Center in Buffalo."

****

Now to *Buffalo's Voices of Steel*. Its perspective is that the people who made steel are a powerful collection of voices about an important, if often overlooked, aspect of our region's history and people.

According to its producers, *Buffalo's Voices of Steel* captures the legacy of the steel industry in Western New York through the voices of the people that worked in the mills. They offer the view that, through reminiscences and remembrances of steel workers, *Buffalo's Voices of Steel* highlights the pride Western New York still feels about its steel producing past.

How did it happen that the two projects, mine much the lesser, come together? I think that Andy and John Grant were aware of the pieces I had written for *The Buffalo News* and the *Pittsburgh Post-Gazette* about Bethlehem's Lackawanna plant. Andy invited me to record my thoughts for the program, which I did. I traveled from Naples, FL, to Washington, DC, and the Channel 17 TV production team drove from Buffalo to Washington, to record what remarks I had to make about my own experience in March 2010. My remembrances were then added to the 20 plus other interviews done for "*Buffalo's Voices of Steel.*"

WNED TV, the PBS television in Buffalo and Toronto, has produced a program, *Buffalo's Voices of Steel* that reaches back into history to keep alive the memory of the steel industry as a major part of Western New York's economic and cultural identity for more than 100 years.

The TV station's executives and creative staff have done a meticulous job in capturing what it meant to work in the Buffalo steel mills. This new program encourages people to pay attention to the history of Western New York.

We know by now what happens when we ignore history. I paraphrase a philosopher friend of mine, Robert Sokolowski of Catholic University: The people who worked in factories had qualities we could use right now.

Endnotes

[1] Charles Spencer, *Blue Collar: An Internal Examination of the Workplace.* Chicago: Lakeside Charter Books, 1977.

[2] *Inforplease.com, Steel Industry*, p. 1.

[3] *The Wall Street Journal, Marketplace*, "Steelmakers Crank Up Output", June 1, 2010, p. 1.

[4] "Forging America, The Story of Bethlehem Steel", *The Morning Call*, 2003, p. 111.

[5] *Wikipedia*, definition of a puddler.

[6] "Forging America", in *The Morning Call*, 2003, p. 112.

[7] Ibid. p. 10.

[8] *The Basilica of Our Lady of Victory, 1851 - 1976*, published by Monarch Publishing, Inc., 1976, p. 6 of the un-numbered pages of the document.

[9] The material in these five paragraphs are derivative of the history of Bethlehem Steel, 1840-2003, in *The Morning Call*, p. 112.

[10] *Lackawanna History*, supplied by the Lackawanna Chamber of Commerce and edited by the Rev. Robert McCartney, last modified, 05/02/2004.

[11] *Lackawanna Diamond Jubilee, 1909 - 1984*, A Presentation to the Citizens of Lackawanna, New York, Sponsored by The City of Lackawanna 75th Anniversary Committee, Inc., pp. 13 - 15.

[12] An excellent book, hard to find, is *From Fire To Rust: Business Technology and Work at the Lackawanna Steel Plant, 1899 - 1983*, by Thomas Leary and Elizabeth C. Sholes, published by Buffalo & Erie County Historical Society in 1987. It gives insight, among other things, into why evolving technologies led to the shutdown of the plant.

[13] *Wikipedia* entry describing the move of the Lackawanna Iron and Steel Company.

[14] *"Lackawanna History"* p. 3 of 3.

[15] *Wikipedia* entry of the Lackawanna Iron and Steel Company.

[16] Ibid. p. 2 of 3.

[17] Ibid. p. 3 of 3.

[18] In 2005, I discussed the Cortland post card with a good friend and cousin by marriage, Mary Cantlin Lalley. Mary told me that her mother was from Cortland. Her grandparents, Maggie and Pat Moran Keefe, born in Ireland, married in Cortland - at St. Mary's Church - and lived at 93 Lincoln Avenue. Pat Keefe worked for the railroad. This address is a few blocks from where my grandmother lived for a time. Cortland was a small place. Perhaps they knew each other.

[19] *Wikipedia* entry.

[20] *Lackawanna Diamond Jubilee, 1909 - 1984*, p. 17

[21] *The Buffalo News*, November 1, 2009.

[22] *Lackawanna's Diamond Jubilee*, p. 34.

[23] *South Bend Tribune*, October 23, 1999, Partial Obituary of Rev. Robert Griffin C.S.C., Oct. 7, 1925 -Oct. 20, 1999, follows:

Rev. Robert Griffin, C.S.C., died at 12:30 p.m. on Wednesday, Oct. 20, in Holy Cross House at the University of Notre Dame. He was 74 years old and had been in ill health for some time.

One of Notre Dame's most affectionate and affectionately regarded characters, the chain-smoking Father Griffin, invariably accompanied by a golden cocker spaniel named Darby O'Gill, was a ubiquitous campus presence for three decades."

[24] In later years, I held positions in the U.S. Congress, Labor Department, Treasury Department and United Nations as well as in private industry.

[25] Ibid. pp. 34-38.

[26] Open Hearth Steelmaking

In 1865, Emile Martin and Pierre Martin took out a license from Siemens and first applied his furnace for making steel. Their process was known as the Siemens-Martin process, and the furnace as an "open-hearth" furnace. The rapid production of large quantities of basic steel was essential, for example, to construct tall buildings. It is the most appealing characteristic of the Siemens regenerative furnace. The usual size of furnaces is 50 to 100 tons, but for special purposes, they may have a capacity of 250 tons or even 500 tons. The Siemens-Martin process complemented rather than replacing the *Bessemer process*. It was slower and thus easier to control. - Wikipedia

[27] *Steel; The Diary Of A Furnace Worker*, Charles R. (Charles Rumford) Walker, The Atlantic Monthly Press, 1922, p. V.

[27] Ibid. p. 35.

[29] Op. cit. p. 35.

[30] "The Next Page, a story of a steel-driven man" in the *Pittsburgh Post-Gazette*, March 8, 2009.

[31] Ibid. pp. 34-38.

[32] "Sunday Forum: Patronage Time: "After the selection comes the hiring of the hacks. Michael D. Langan looks back on his 'work' as a civil servant." *Pittsburgh Post-Gazette*, November 16, 2008.

[33] Ibid.

[34] "At Closing Plant, Ordeal Included Heart Attacks", by Michael Luo in *The New York Times*, February 25, 2010, p.1.

[35] Ibid. p. 1

[36] *City Without A Pulse*, John Strohmeyer, APF Reporter, p. 1 of 7.

[37] *The Last Fine Time,* Verlyn Klinkenborg, Alfred A. Knopf, 1991, pp. 91-92.

[38] John Strohmeyer, *Rebuilding Bethlehem Steel.*

[39] John Strohmeyer, *City Without A Pulse.*

[40] Ibid.

[41] John Strohmeyer, *Rebuilding Bethlehem Steel.*

[42] *Bethlehem Steel, 1840 - 2003*, "Forging America: The Story of Bethlehem Steel", *The Morning Call*, Allentown, PA newspaper, copyright 2010.

Bibliography

The *Basilica of Our Lady of Victory" 1851 - 1976*, Monarch Publishing, Inc., 1976.

Crisis In Bethlehem, Big Steel's Struggle To Survive, John Strohmeyer, University of Pittsburgh Press, 1986.

"The Next Page, a story of a steel-driven man" in the *Pittsburgh Post-Gazette*, March 8, 2009.

City On The Edge, Buffalo, New York, by Mark Goldman, Prometheus Books, 2007.

City Without A Pulse, John Strohmeyer, APF Reporter,

First Helper's Instructional Manual, Bethlehem Steel, Lackawanna Plant, January 1958.

"Forging America, The Story Of Bethlehem Steel", *The Morning Call*, 2003.

From Fire to Rust, Business, Technology and Work at the Lackawanna Steel Plant, 1899 - 1983, Thomas E. Leary and Elizabeth C. Sholes, published by the Buffalo and Erie County Historical Society, 1987.

Lackawanna Diamond Jubilee, 1909 - 1984, A Presentation to the Citizens of Lackawanna, New York Sponsored by The City of Lackawanna 75th Anniversary Committee, Inc., 1984.

Lackawanna History, supplied by the Lackawanna Chamber of Commerce and edited by the Rev. Robert McCartney, last modified, 05/02/2004.

Steel; The Diary Of A Furnace Worker, Charles R. (Charles Rumford) Walker, The Atlantic Monthly Press, 1922.

Sunday Forum: Patronage Time "After the selection comes the hiring of the hacks. Michael D. Langan looks back on his 'work' as a civil servant", *Pittsburgh Post-Gazette*, November 16, 2008.

The Last Fine Time, Verlyn Klinkenborg, Alfred A. Knopf, 1991.

Out of This Furnace, A Novel of Immigrant Labor in America, Thomas Bell, University of Pittsburg Press, 1976.

Source Acknowledgements

I extend my thanks for use of published material in this book that I have written and had earlier appeared in *The Buffalo News* and the *Pittsburgh Post-Gazette*.

Special Thanks

Certain people encouraged or enabled me to write "Tapping Out", and I want to thank them. They include my 'first helper' for 51 years, a wonderful editor and thoughtful contributor, Joanne Ernst Langan.

Thanks too, to my children, Joanne Cleary, Jeanne Burris and Michael D. Langan for their support. I appreciate the generous help of Bill Cleary, my son-in-law, and Dr. Joseph F. Bieron, my old (literally) classmate, who guided the book through its production. I acknowledge the valuable help of Don Williams, Vice President of the Steel Plant Museum; Mike Malyak, Recording Secretary of the Steel Plant Museum; Nancy Weekly and Scott Propeack of the Burchfield-Penney Art Museum; Andy and John Grant of Driftwood Productions; and Bill McShane, retired superintendent of #2 open hearth.